Workbook

Caroline Nixon and Michael Tomlinson

T0392211

CAMBRIDGE
UNIVERSITY PRESS

Map of the book

Meet the family

1 **Read and write the words.**

> eight   fine   His   live   meet   name   ~~old~~

1 How _old_ are you?

I'm _____ .

2 How are you?
I'm _____ , thanks.

3 What's your _____ ?

My name's Vicky.

4 Where do you _____ ?

I live in Boston.

5 Hi. I'm Jane.
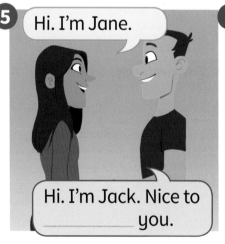
Hi. I'm Jack. Nice to _____ you.

6 What's his name?
_____ name's Peter.

2 🎧 5.02 **Listen and write.**

Name: _Jack_

Last name: _____

Age: _____

Address number: _____

Street: _____

Town: _____

1 🎧 5.03 Listen and number. Then listen again and write.

a ☐
_____

b ☐
_____

c ☐
_____

d ☐
_____

e 1
Cameron

f ☐
_____

2 Match. Draw lines with the right color.

1	Is Harry's dad big? (black)	a	Yes, she does.
2	Is the picture of Shelly's brother? (blue)	b	Yes, she is.
3	Can Shelly sing? (red)	c	Yes, he is.
4	Is Rocky's mother asleep? (orange)	d	No, he doesn't.
5	Does Gracie like eating paper? (pink)	e	No, he isn't.
6	Is Harry's dad sad? (purple)	f	No, she can't.
7	Does Cameron like Shelly's singing? (green)	g	No, it isn't.

1 A day on the farm

My unit goals

Practice	Say and write	Learn to say
	 **8** **10** **12** new words in English	in English

My mission diary

	Hooray!	OK	Try again
1			
2			
3			
★			

My favorite stage: _____

Go to page 134 and add to your word stack!

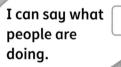

☐ I can name things in the country.

☐ I can say what people are doing.

☑ I can write about my daily routines.

☐ I can say what's different in two pictures.

①

1 Read and match.

a

b

c

d 1

e

f

g

h

1 Vicky and Charlie are sitting next to the lake.

2 It's a nice day. Let's go for a walk in the forest.

3 Jane's fishing in the river with her grandma.

4 Look at those cows in that field.

5 Lily and Jack are playing on the grass.

6 There are a lot of yellow and brown leaves under that tree.

7 My dog is digging in the ground.

8 There's a big mountain behind Fred's house.

Sounds and spelling

How do we say this letter?

r

2 🎧 5.04 **Listen and ⟨circle⟩ the words with a /r/ sound. Then listen again and match.**

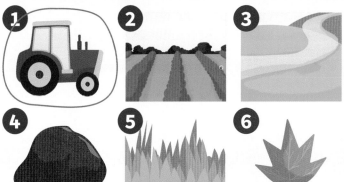

1 2 3 4 5 6

a leaf ☐
b river ☐
c rock ☐
d grass ☐
e tractor 1
f field ☐

The Friendly Farm

1 🎧 5.05 **Listen and circle the correct words.**

1 Rocky's *talking* / *singing* to Cameron and Henrietta.

2 The kittens *are* / *aren't* sleeping.

3 The mother cat's washing the kitten's *legs* / *face*.

4 The puppy with the short tail is *playing* / *eating*.

5 The big puppy's looking at its *tail* / *face*.

6 The fat puppy's *eating* / *washing* the red sock.

2 **Talk about the pictures. Use the words from the box.**

> drinking   eating   looking   playing   sleeping

> Look at the fat puppy. It's eating a red sock.

1 Read and match. Color.

1 Fred's eating	3 Vicky's mom's taking	their shoes.	a picture.
2 Daisy's washing	4 Mary and Paul are cleaning	her face.	an ice cream.

2 Answer the questions.

1 Are the puppies sleeping?

No, they aren't.

2 Is the kitten playing?

_____

3 Is the girl eating sausages?

_____

4 Are the children walking?

_____

5 Is the boy washing his hands?

_____

6 Is the bird singing?

_____

7 Is the woman putting on her shoes?

_____

8 Is the man driving a car?

_____

1 Write the words. Find the secret word.

1 He **tegs** _gets_ up at eight o'clock.

2 She takes a **wesohr** _____ in the evening.

3 I put **ttthpsaeoo** _____ on my toothbrush.

4 I brush my **hetet** _____ at night.

5 My dad **sha** _____ cereal with milk for breakfast.

6 I have **asefatrkb** _____ at nine o'clock.

7 I get **redseds** _____ in the morning.

8 I love chicken and rice for **chlnu** _____ .

9 My mom **skwea** _____ up at seven o'clock.

10 My sister **sshewa** _____ her hands before lunch.

¹g	e	t	s					
2								
3								
		4						
		5						
		6						
	7							
	8							
9								
10								

What's the secret word?

_____

2 🎧 5.06 Listen and check (✓).

1 What's the kitten doing?

a   b ✓   c

2 What's Peter doing now?

a   b   c

3 What color is Charlie's toothbrush?

a   b   c

4 What does Daisy have for breakfast today?

a   b   c

1 Write the words in the correct order.

1 at seven / wakes up / Jack / o'clock / .

Jack wakes up at seven o'clock.

2 Do the / dinner with / their family / children have / ?

_____

3 school / have / Jim doesn't / lunch at / .

_____

4 Sally have / Does / her mom / breakfast with / ?

_____

5 school at / nine o'clock / Mary / goes to / .

_____

6 Charlie brush / the bathroom / their teeth in / Peter and / .

_____

2 Read and write the words.

> breakfast   brushes   dressed   gets   o'clock   ~~up~~   takes   walks

Vicky wakes [1] ___up___ at seven o'clock every day. She [2] _____ up and goes to the bathroom. She [3] _____ a shower and gets [4] _____ . She has [5] _____ with her dad in the kitchen. Then she [6] _____ her teeth and goes to school. She [7] _____ to school with her mom. School starts at nine [8] _____ . Vicky loves school.

1 Check (✓) the things that are good for the Earth.

1

✓

2

3

4

5

6

2 Read and write *yes* or *no*.

1 People can live on all the planets in our solar system. _no_

2 We can live on Earth because there is water and air. _____

3 Living things need plastic to live. _____

4 Dirty air and water are bad for the planet and for us. _____

5 Everybody needs to help take care of the planet. _____

Learn about how to take care of our planet

3 **Which is better for the Earth? Look and check (✓).**

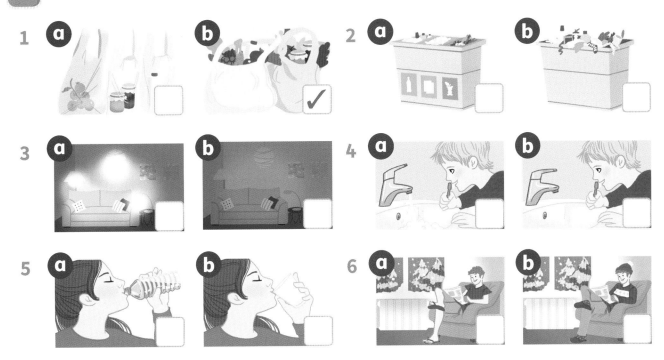

4 **How can we take care of our planet? Draw and write.**

1 **Read and circle the correct answer.**

1 Where are Beth and Gwen? a (at home) b in school

2 Who do they go to see? a a dog named Jess b a friend called Jess

3 Where does the dog play? a in the kitchen b in the field

4 Who falls over? a Beth b Gwen

5 Why does Gwen stop running? a she wins the race b to help her sister

2 **Read the sentences. Write *yes* or *no*. Explain your answers.**

1 Beth wants to see Jess.

   yes   The poem says, "Come on, Gwen!" says
   Beth. "Let's go and see Jess!"

2 Jess is an old dog.

_____

3 Beth and Gwen see Jess every day.

_____

4 Beth falls on the ground.

_____

5 Gwen doesn't help her sister.

_____

3 **What do you enjoy doing with your family? Write, then talk with a friend.**

I like _____

_____

> I like going swimming with my family!

4 🎧 5.07 **Listen and draw lines.**

Kim   Sally   Peter   Mary

John   Lily   Nick

1 🎧 5.08 Find four differences.

1 Play the game.

What's this? | It's a toothbrush.

START	What's this? 	What are these? 	What's she doing? 	What are these? 
What's this? 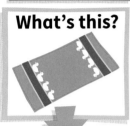	What's this? 	What's he doing? 	What are these? 	TAKE ANOTHER TURN
What's this? 	What's she doing? 	MISS A TURN	What's this? 	What are they doing? 
TAKE ANOTHER TURN	What are these? 	What's this? 	What are these? 	What are these? 
What's this? 	What's he doing? 	What are these? 	MISS A TURN	What's this? 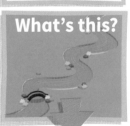
FINISH	What's she doing? 	What are these? 	What are they doing? 	What's he doing? 

INSTRUCTIONS

1 Roll the die and move your marker.

2 Answer the question.

17

2 My week

My unit goals

Practice

Say and write
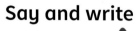
8 10 12
new words in English

Learn to say

in English

My  mission diary

	Hooray!	OK	Try again
1			
2			
3			
★			

My favorite stage: _____

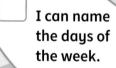
Go to page 134 and add to your word stack!

☐ I can name the days of the week.

☐ I can ask and answer questions with *How often … ?*

☐ I can talk about free-time activities.

☐ I can read sentences and copy English words.

1 Read and write the words.

> Friday   ~~Monday~~   Saturday   Sunday
> Thursday   Tuesday   Wednesday   weekend

1 Sunday comes between Saturday and _____Monday_____ .

2 Friday comes after _____ .

3 Tuesday comes before _____ .

4 Thursday comes between Wednesday and _____ .

5 Monday comes before _____ .

6 Saturday and Sunday are the _____ .

7 Monday comes after _____ .

8 The weekend is _____ and Sunday.

Sounds and spelling

How do we say these letters?

2 🎧 5.09 Listen and say the rhyme.

On Mond**ay** and Tuesd**ay**,
I don't pl**ay**.

On Wednesd**ay** and
Thursd**ay**, I do.

On Frid**ay** and Saturd**ay**,
I pl**ay** all d**ay**.

On Sund**ay**, I pl**ay** at
the zoo!

1 🎧 5.10 Listen and complete the sentences.

1 Let's put Fred here on
   <u>   the table   </u>.

2 Jim and Jenny have a
   _____.

3 How often do they
   _____?

4 How often does it wash
   _____?

5 I don't know. No, I don't
   _____.

6 I sometimes talk, but I never talk
   _____!

2 Circle the word that is true for you. Write, then tell your friend.

1 I *sometimes / always / never* play tennis on the weekend.

2 I *sometimes / always / never* do my homework in school.

3 I *sometimes / always / never* watch TV on Wednesdays.

4 I sometimes _____.

5 I always _____.

6 I never _____.

> I sometimes play tennis on the weekend.

1 **Read and write the words.**

| before | ~~has~~ | evening | kitten | never | plays | sometimes |

Vicky ¹ _has_ a new kitten. His name is
Simba. Vicky always feeds him ² _____
breakfast in the morning and after dinner in
the ³ _____ . She often ⁴ _____
with him before school. They love playing.
Simba likes sleeping in the sun. He often
sleeps in the yard, but when there's no sun he
⁵ _____ sleeps in his bed in the living
room. He's ⁶ _____ naughty – he's a
very good ⁷ _____ .

2 **Join and write the sentences.**

1 She doesn't	never eats	he play	before lunch.
2 They always	our	their	every day.
3 How often	wash	listen to	homework after school?
4 She	often	their hands	for breakfast.
5 We feed	does	hamburgers	in the park?
6 Do they	always do	puppy twice	the radio.

1 She doesn't often listen to the radio. _____

2 _____

3 _____

4 _____

5 _____

6 _____

1 Look and write the words.

go shopping   go skating   listen to a CD   listen to music
read a comic book   watch a DVD   watch movies   write an email

listen to a CD

2 Look at the pictures in Activity 1. Complete the sentences.

1 When I do my homework, I never listen to ___music___ on the radio.

2 Every Saturday, May _____ a movie at the theater with her mom.

3 Jane enjoys reading _____. Her mom buys her favorite one every Friday afternoon.

4 We _____ in town every weekend to buy things.

5 I never listen to music on the radio. I always _____ a CD in my bedroom.

6 We like to take our skates and _____ in the park.

7 I sometimes write an _____ to my cousin. He lives in a different town.

8 I never go to the movie theater. I watch _____ at home.

1 Read and write the words.

Sally enjoys reading comic books. She gets a new ¹ _comic book_ every Saturday morning, and she reads it in her ² _____ before lunch. She goes shopping with her ³ _____ every Saturday afternoon. They always go to the same ⁴ _____ to buy their fruit. Today, they're buying ⁵ _____ . Sally's very happy. They're her favorite fruit.

books

bedroom

~~comic book~~

dad

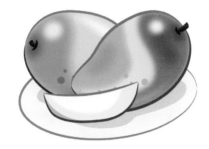

mangoes

store

2 Read and match.

1	We should study	a	her homework after school.
2	What should you do	b	his dirty shoes on the sofa.
3	He should not put	c	buy milk at the store.
4	They should not eat	d	for our exams.
5	She should do	e	our hands before we eat.
6	We should always wash	f	when you are sick?
7	I should	g	candy in class.

1 Draw the things that are missing in the picture.

2 Read and write the names.

Daisy

_____

_____

_____

_____

_____

Sally is wearing gloves and a helmet. Nick has goggles and a towel.
Jane is wearing goggles, gloves, and a helmet. Charlie is wearing gloves.
Daisy is wearing a helmet and gloves. John is wearing a helmet, knee
pads, and elbow pads.

3 Write.

When I _____, I wear _____.

Learn about being safe when exercising and playing sports

4 **Who is taking care of their bodies? Look and check (✓).**

5 **Complete the sentences with the words from the box.**

> clothes   drink   helmet   ~~muscles~~   sunblock   water

1   It is important to warm up our __muscles__ before we exercise.

2   When we get hot, our body loses _____. So it's important to _____ lots when we play sports.

3   We should use _____ to protect our skin from the sun.

4   It is important to wear the correct _____ when we play sports.

5   We should wear a _____ when we ride a bike or go skating.

1 **Read the story again. Complete the notes.**

Name of the story: A bad, bad Monday morning

Main character

Name: _____

What's he like? _____

How do you know? _____

Where and when?

At the beginning: _____

In the middle: _____

At the end: _____

2 **Check (✓) the best answer.**

The story is about:

a   Alex's presentation at school.   ☐

b   What happens when Alex doesn't get up on time.   ☐

c   Alex's favorite day of the week.   ☐

3 **Can you think of ways to help Alex with his problem?**

_____

_____

4 🎧 5.11 Listen and check (✓).

1 When are the soccer matches?

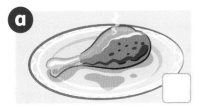 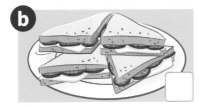 

2 What does the boy want?

3 What does the boy want to do?

4 Who is the girl's P.E. teacher?

5 Where are the children?

6 What is the boy looking for?

1 **Look and read. Choose the correct words and write them on the lines. There is one example.**

an email

movies

rocks

a forest

a comic book

grass

a lake

roller-skating

Example

Lizards like to sit on these when the sun is out.   _rocks_

Questions

1   You find this in the yard on the ground.   _____

2   Some people write this on a computer.   _____

3   There are lots of trees in this place.   _____

4   You can watch these at home on your TV.   _____

5   This is in the country and you often see fish here.   _____

1 Play the game.

I always read comic books on Saturdays.

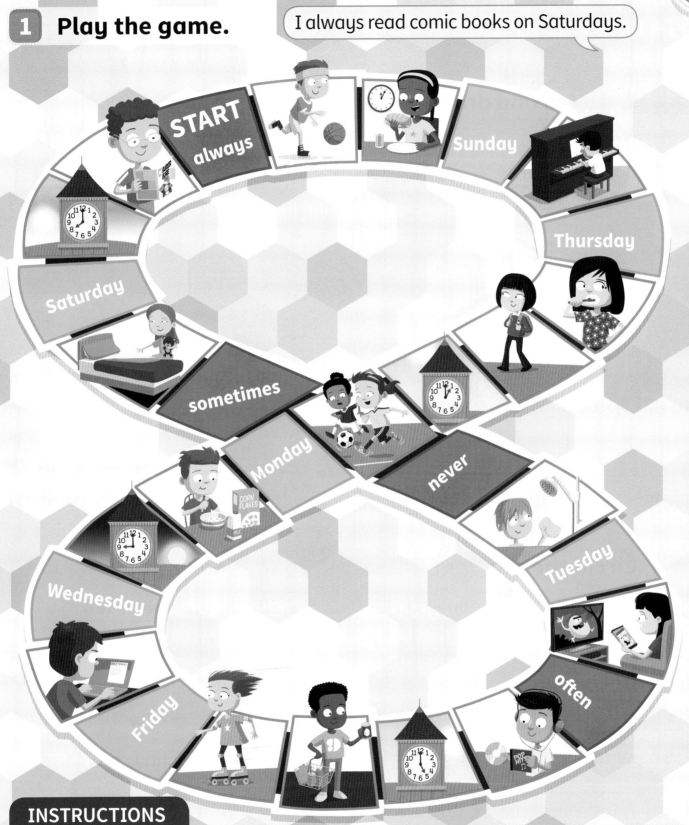

INSTRUCTIONS

1 Look at the words and pictures and write four sentences.

2 Roll the die and move your marker.

3 Collect your words.

4 Say your sentences.

Review ••• Units 1–2

1 🎧 5.12 Listen and draw lines.

Monday   Tuesday   Wednesday   Thursday   Friday

2 Circle the one that doesn't belong. Say why.

1 Tuesday	Wednesday	Friday	weekend
2 clown	watch a movie	listen to music	go skating
3 toothpaste	toothbrush	bed	towel
4 farm	sea	lake	river
5 go to bed	wake up	get dressed	have breakfast

The word "weekend" is different.

Why?

Because it's not a day.

3 Look and read. Write *yes* or *no*.

1	A kitten is eating flowers.	*no*
2	A farmer is wearing dirty boots in the house.	_____
3	A big puppy is eating a toothbrush.	_____
4	A big puppy is sleeping on the TV.	_____
5	A boy is eating lunch with clean hands.	_____
6	A cook is walking on the table.	_____
7	A girl is riding a bike.	_____

4 Look at the picture in Activity 3 and complete the sentences. Use *should / should not* and a word from the box.

eat (x2)   ~~sleep~~   walk   wash   wear (x2)

1 The big puppy _should not sleep_ on the TV.

2 The farmer _____ dirty boots in the house.

3 The small puppy _____ the toothbrush.

4 The puppy _____ the flowers.

5 The boy _____ his hands before he eats his lunch.

6 The orange kitten _____ on the table.

7 The girl _____ a helmet when she rides her bike.

3 Party time!

My unit goals

Practice	Say and write	Learn to say
	8 10 12 new words in English	in English

My mission diary

	Hooray!	OK	Try again
1	:)	:|	:~
2	:)	:|	:~
3	:)	:|	:~
★	:)	:|	:~

My favorite stage: _____

Go to page 134 and add to your word stack!

I can name jobs and things at a party.

I can talk about what people look like.

I can ask and answer questions with *Why ... ?* and *Because ...*

I can use pictures to tell a story.

1 **Write the words. Find the secret word.**

What is the secret word? _____

Sounds and spelling

2 🎧 5.13 **Can you hear the /ɑ:/ sound? Listen and say *yes* or *no*.**

3 🎧 5.14 **Listen and color the letters that make the /ɑ:/ sound.**

How do we write that sound?

father
grandpa
grandma

party
farmer
movie star

1 🎧 5.15 **Listen, read, and correct.**

1   Cameron's wearing a ~~dentist~~ costume from the party.   _____clown_____

2   Farmer Friendly's outside feeding the sheep.   _____

3   Shelly wants to be a pop star.   _____

4   Gracie likes studying. She can be a pirate.   _____

5   Doctors help other clowns.   _____

6   Gracie wants to look at Harry's hat.   _____

2 **Read and write the words.**

> ~~feeding~~   helping   wants   wear

1   Grandpa always feeds the cows in the evening. He's __feeding__ them now.

2   Cameron's wearing a clown costume. He doesn't often _____ clothes.

3   Doctors always help people. Gracie's _____ Harry.

4   Movie stars often go to parties. Shelly _____ to be a movie star.

③

1   Read and circle the correct words.

1   It's eight o'clock now. Charlie *is taking* / *takes* a shower.

2   Vicky *is having* / *has* dinner at eight o'clock every day.

3   Jim and Daisy often *are playing* / *play* tennis on the weekend.

4   Sally never *is wearing* / *wears* a dress.

5   Fred's in the bathroom. He *'s washing* / *washes* his face.

6   Mary and Jane sometimes *are skating* / *skate* in the park after school.

7   It's bedtime. Peter *'s getting* / *gets* undressed.

8   Vicky loves swimming. She always *is going* / *goes* for a swim on Saturdays.

2   Read and write the names.

_____   _____   _____   Jim _____

My dad never watches TV in the morning. He makes my breakfast. His name is Jim, and he's making my breakfast now.

My friend has a fish. She feeds it every morning. She isn't feeding it now. She's skateboarding. Her name's Vicky.

My brother always wears jeans and a T-shirt on the weekend, but today he's at a party. He's wearing a dentist costume. His name's Paul.

My sister Lily loves skateboarding, but she isn't skateboarding now. She's doing her homework.

1 🎧 5.16 **Listen and number.**

a

b

c  1

d

e

f

2 **Look, read, and write.**

Complete the sentences.

1 The pirate has a long, black _____beard_____ .

2 The tall clown has purple, curly _____.

Answer the questions.

3 What's the boy with the straight, blond hair? _____

4 What are the clowns doing? _____

5 Now write a sentence about the picture.

_____

③

1 Write the words in the correct order.

1 brushing / his teeth / Why's / he / ?
   Why's he brushing his teeth?

2 a movie star / I'm taking / because she's /
   pictures of her / .
   _____

3 tennis because / They can't play / have a ball /
   they don't / .
   _____

4 She's wearing / because she's / a helmet /
   riding a horse / .
   _____

5 happy today / because it's / Peter's very / his birthday / .
   _____

6 a costume party / wearing costumes / because they're at / They're / .
   _____

2 Match the questions with the answers.

1 Why's he getting his swimsuit
   and towel?

2 Why aren't the children
   in school?

3 Why's she wearing a helmet?

4 Why's he writing an email to
   his friends?

5 Why's she cleaning her shoes?

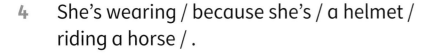

a Because they're dirty.

b Because she's roller-skating.

c Because it's Tuesday. He always
   goes for a swim on Tuesdays.

d Because it's the weekend and
   they don't have classes.

e Because he's inviting them to
   his party.

1 Write the words.

1

chtaeer

t e a c h e r

2

lipoce iceroff

_ _ _ _ _ _ _ _ _ _ _ _ _

3

rooctd

_ _ _ _ _ _

4

ersnu

_ _ _ _ _

5

erfighitfer

_ _ _ _ _ _ _ _ _ _ _

6

isetdnt

_ _ _ _ _ _ _

2 Look, read, and match.

1	He's	a	in a hospital.
2	He works	b	sick children.
3	He wears	c	a nurse.
4	He takes care of	d	a blue uniform.
5	She's a	e	traffic.
6	She works	f	police officer.
7	She wears	g	in a police station.
8	She directs the	h	a black uniform.

Learn about people who help us at home, in school, and in the community

3 Who can help? Look and write the words.

1

police officer

2

_____

3

_____

4

_____

4 Read and write the words.

dentist   ~~doctor~~   farmer   firefighter   police officer   teacher

1 This person takes care of people in a hospital. _____doctor_____

2 This person directs the traffic. _____

3 This person puts out fires. _____

4 This person teaches children. _____

5 This person makes sure your teeth are OK. _____

6 This person works with animals and plants. _____

1 Answer the questions.

1 Who's having a costume party? Why?

   Emily's having a costume party because _it's her birthday_ .

2 What costume does Matt want?

   Matt really wants a _____ costume.

3 Why does his mother think a pirate costume is a good idea?

   Matt can make a beard and has a pirate _____ .

4 What is Matt's costume in the end?

   It's a _____ .

2 Complete the sentences.

   beard ~~costume~~ funny pirate pop superhero

1 Everyone needs a _costume_ for Emily's party.

2 Harry has a _____ costume for the party, but he can't fly!

3 Matt can make a _____ and a mustache.

4 He has a _____ hat.

5 Emily sings because she is a _____ star at her party.

6 Everyone laughs at Matt's costume because he looks very _____ .

3 Ask your friends for ideas, then draw your costume for Emily's party in your notebook.

Can you help me think of a costume for the party?

What about a _____ ?

4 Look, read, and write.

a party

a farmer

~~a superhero~~

a sheep

a hat

a mustache

1 This person is in comic books and movies and on TV   <u>a superhero</u>

2 People wear this on their heads.   _____

3 You have this when it's your birthday.   _____

4 This person takes care of animals or grows vegetables, grains, or fruit.   _____

5 This animal has a thick, white, curly coat.   _____

1 5.17 Tell the story.

Mary and Zoe are pop stars.

Mary **Zoe**

3

1 Play the game.

INSTRUCTIONS

1 Roll the die and move your marker.

2 Describe the person.

The farmer's tall. He has light hair and a mustache.

4 The family at home

My unit goals

Practice

Say and write

8 10 12

new words in English

Learn to say

in English

My mission diary

	Hooray!	OK	Try again
1	😊	😐	😕
2	😊	😐	😕
3	😊	😐	😕
⭐	😊	😐	😕

My favorite stage: _____

Go to page 134 and add to your word stack!

I can understand when someone talks about their family.

I can compare people and things.

I can talk about people's homes.

I can listen and match people to pictures.

1 Write the words.

1 Zoe is Jim and Jenny's **nicsou** _____cousin_____ .

2 Jack is Jim and Jenny's **lecnu** _____ .

3 Jenny is Mr. Friendly's **ghtaured** _____ .

4 Jim is Mrs. Friendly's **nso** _____ .

5 Julia is Jim and Jenny's **tuna** _____ .

6 Jim is Grandma Friendly's **snogradn** _____ .

7 Jenny is Grandpa Friendly's **rddtganuergha** _____ .

8 Mr. and Mrs. Friendly are Jim and Jenny's **snetrap** _____ .

9 Grandma and Grandpa Friendly are Zoe's **strapnendrag** _____ .

Sounds and spelling

2 🎧 5.18 **Can you hear the /ʌ/ sound? Listen and say *yes* or *no*.**

How do we write that sound?

3 🎧 5.19 **Listen and color the letters that make the /ʌ/ sound.**

mother
brother son

uncle

cousin

The Friendly Farm

1 🎧 5.20 **Listen, read, and write a check (✓) or an ✗.**

1   It's funnier than the family picture in the living room.   ✓

2   Jim and Jenny's uncle is shorter than their dad.   ☐

3   Jim and Jenny's cousin is bigger and older than them.   ☐

4   Gracie's ears are shorter than Shelly's.   ☐

5   Shelly's feet are smaller and cleaner than Gracie's.   ☐

6   The animals should all be nicer to everyone.   ☐

2 **Write sentences. Talk with your friends.**

> bigger   older   prettier   smaller   thinner   younger

_____

_____

_____

_____

Rocky's younger than Henrietta.

1 **Write the comparatives.**

~~angry~~ ~~bad~~ ~~big~~ curly fat good happy ~~long~~ naughty
sad short straight tall thin ugly young

+er	y̶ +ier	double letter +er	irregular
longer	angrier	bigger	worse

2 **Join and write the sentences.**

1 My mom's hair's   are thinner   better than   dog's tail.

2 The cat's tail's   beard's shorter   than my uncle's   our old one.

3 The kittens   curlier than   than the   beard.

4 My dad's   house is   than   aunt's hair.

5 Our new   longer   my   the puppies.

1   My mom's hair's curlier than my aunt's hair.

2   _____

3   _____

4   _____

5   _____

1 (Circle) the one that doesn't belong. Say why.

A town is not part of your house.

1 basement	roof	(town)	balcony
2 clown	first floor	dentist	nurse
3 city	stairs	country	town
4 doctor	second floor	first floor	third floor
5 lake	field	basement	river
6 straight	curly	roof	light
7 beard	town	mustache	hair
8 son	daughter	parents	balcony
9 basement	present	cake	costume
10 movie	DVD	TV	downstairs

2 🎧 5.21 **Listen and write a letter in each box.**

his aunt
 c

his uncle

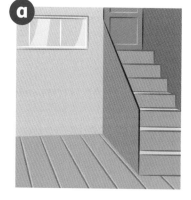
a

b

his grandparents

his parents

c

d

1 **Read and match. Color.**

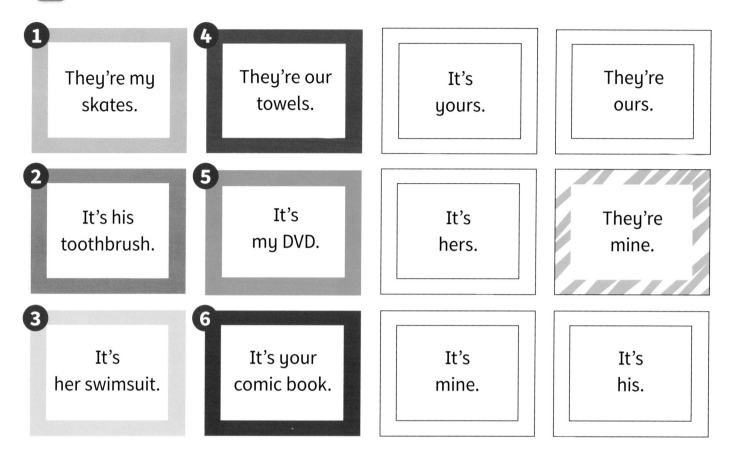

1 They're my skates.

4 They're our towels.

It's yours.

They're ours.

2 It's his toothbrush.

5 It's my DVD.

It's hers.

They're mine.

3 It's her swimsuit.

6 It's your comic book.

It's mine.

It's his.

2 **Read and (circle) the correct words.**

1 **A** Is that your grandpa's tractor?

B Yes, it's *his* / *hers*.

2 **A** Vicky, Jane, where are your shoes?

B *Mine / Theirs* are next to the stairs and *his / hers* are in the closet.

3 **A** Is that the pirates' treasure?

B Yes, it's *theirs / mine*.

4 **A** Are these CDs yours or your dad's?

B They're *his / hers*.

5 **A** Is this book mine or yours?

B It's *his / yours*.

1 Look and match the machine to the problem.

2 Where do we use these machines? Write the words.

in the park   in the classroom   in the house   on the street

1 in the house

2 _____

3 _____

4 _____

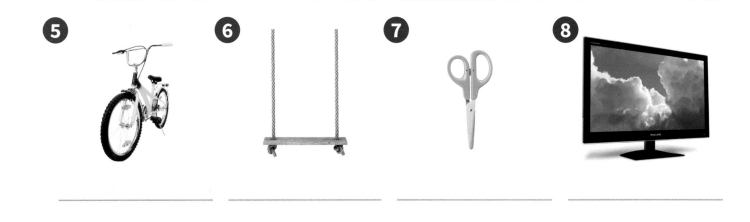

5 _____

6 _____

7 _____

8 _____

3 Look at Activity 4. Number the pictures.

a

b 1

c

d

e

f

g

h

4 Do you help at home? Write a check (✓) or an ✗. Then ask your friends.

		You			
1	Do you set the table?				
2	Do you do the dishes or load the dishwasher?				
3	Do you make your bed?				
4	Do you clean your room?				
5	Do you water the plants?				
6	Do you help your parents cook?				
7	Do you vacuum the floor?				
8	Do you load the washing machine?				

Do you set the table?   Yes, I do.

1 **Answer the questions.**

1   Whose birthday is it?

It's Max's mom's birthday.

2   What food is there at the party?

_____

3   Why are Uncle Paul and Grandma on the balcony?

_____

4   Why is Max's mom late?

_____

5   What idea does Max have?

_____

2 **Write the words. Act it out with a friend.**

~~Mom~~   party   phone   train

Max: Where is ¹ _____Mom_____ ?

Uncle Paul: I don't know, Max.

Max: She's very late. We can't have the ² _____ without her.

Uncle Paul: Is she on the ³ _____ home?

Max: Maybe.

Uncle Paul: Max! That's the ⁴ _____ ! Quick!

3 **What do you do for your birthday? Do you have a big party? Tell your friend.**

I like watching DVDs with my friends and then having a big party at home!

4 Look, read, and write.

1   Mom is wearing a green _____hat_____ .

2   Marta and Juan are reading _____ .

3   Uncle Paul is drinking some _____ .

4   What is Max's dad wearing?

_____

5   Where is the ball?

_____

6   What is Max doing?

_____

7   Now write two sentences about the picture.

_____

_____

1 🎧 5.22 **Listen and look. There is one example. Lily is telling her teacher about different people in her family and where they live. Which is each person's home?**

 H
her brother

her grandfather

her cousin

her uncle

her aunt

her grandmother

A  **B**  **C**  **D**

E  **F**  **G**  **H**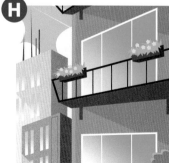

1 Play the game.

It's time for lunch. Go to the dining room.

You help your grandparents make lunch. Go to the kitchen.

Go to the stairs and help your younger cousin go up them.

You want to brush your teeth. Go to the bathroom.

There's a cat asleep on a roof!

Which places are you going to?

balcony
basement
bathroom
bedroom
dining room
hallway
kitchen
living room
roof
stairs
street
yard

Go upstairs to your bedroom.

Today you can play outside. Go to the yard.

Go downstairs to the basement.

Go shopping in the city with your parents.

Your uncle is on the balcony. Go and talk to him.

You want to watch TV. Go to the living room.

Your aunt's here. Go to the hallway to open the door.

Where are you going?

I'm going to the basement.

INSTRUCTIONS

1 Choose a place to start.

2 Check four places on your list.

3 Roll the die and move your marker.

4 Visit the places on your list.

Review ••• Units 3–4

1 🎧 5.23 **Listen and number the machines. Then write.**

> microwave   pencil sharpener   hairdryer
> washing machine   ~~dishwasher~~   vacuum cleaner

a ☐

_____

b ☐

_____

c ☐

_____

d ☐

_____

e 1

dishwasher

f ☐

_____

2 **Read and ⟨circle⟩ the correct words.**

1   I always ⟨help⟩/ *am helping* my dad load the dishwasher after dinner.

2   Alice *dries* / *is drying* her hair right now because her hair *is* / *is being* wet.

3   We sometimes *cook* / *are cooking* our food in the microwave.

4   Aiden *sharpens* / *is sharpening* his pencil because he *broke* / *is breaking* it.

5   You should *vacuum* / *are vacuuming* the floor when it's dirty.

6   They *wash* / *are washing* their clothes every Thursday.

3 **Draw a picture of your home. Use the words in the box to help you. Then show and tell with a friend.**

> balcony   basement   bathroom   bedroom
> dining room   downstairs   fan   floor   hallway
> kitchen   living room   lift   stairs   upstairs   yard

My house has an upstairs, a downstairs, and a big yard.

My apartment doesn't have a yard, but it has a big balcony.

4 **Write about you and your family. Use words from the boxes.**

> aunt   brother   cousin   dad   grandma
> grandpa   mom   sister   uncle

> smart   curly   funny   long   old   short
> straight   tall   young

1   My grandma's hair is curlier than mine.

2   _____

3   _____

4   _____

5   _____

6   _____

5 Animal world

My unit goals

Practice

Say and write

⭐ 8 ⭐ 10 ⭐ 12

new words in English

Learn to say

in English

My mission diary

	Hooray!	OK	Try again
1	🙂	😐	🙁
2	🙂	😐	🙁
3	🙂	😐	🙁
⭐	🙂	😐	🙁

My favorite stage: _____

Go to page 134 and add to your word stack!

I can name wild animals.

I can talk about things animals do.

I can use words like *above* to say where things are.

I can choose the best answers in a conversation.

1 Read and match.

> bat   bear   dolphin   kangaroo   lion   panda
> parrot   ~~penguin~~   rabbit   whale

1   This black and white bird can't fly. _____penguin_____

2   This smart animal lives in the sea. It has a long nose and mouth. _____

3   This small animal sleeps under the ground and jumps a lot. _____

4   This small black and brown animal can fly, but it isn't a bird. _____

5   This is a very big cat. It likes eating and sleeping. _____

6   This beautiful bird has a lot of colors. Sometimes it can speak. _____

7   This big brown and black animal can climb trees and swim. _____

8   This big animal has long legs and short arms. It jumps a lot. _____

9   This black and white bear doesn't eat meat, it eats leaves. _____

10   This gray or black animal is bigger than all other sea animals. _____

Sounds and spelling

2 🎧 5.24 Listen and say. Then listen and match.

How do we say this letter?

goat

giraffe

1 cage   2 kangaroo   3 penguin   4 tiger   5 orange

The Friendly Farm

1 🎧 5.25 **Listen, read, and circle the correct words.**

1   Jim's picture is of a (wildlife) / car park.

2   The bear's *the biggest* / *the smallest*.

3   The kangaroo's *nose* / *tail* is longer than Harry's.

4   Shelly thinks the *parrot* / *bear* is the prettiest.

5   Shelly is *the best* / *the worst* singer in the barn.

6   Rocky says his mom's *the angriest* / *the naughtiest* animal in the barn.

2 **Talk about the animals. Ask and answer with a friend.**

| angriest   biggest   naughtiest   oldest   prettiest   smartest   worst singer |

Who is the worst singer?   Shelly.

1 Read and draw lines.

Three children are looking at the pandas at the zoo. Paul's the oldest and tallest. His sister Vicky's the youngest and shortest. Their sister Sally has the longest hair. It's blond and straight. Sally thinks that the smallest panda is the prettiest of the four. Its name is Chu Lin. Vicky thinks Bao Bao is the happiest, but he's also the dirtiest. The fattest panda is Yang Yang, but he isn't the biggest. Gu Gu is the biggest and the oldest. He's 20 years old.

| Vicky | Chu Lin | Paul | Sally |

| Bao Bao | Yang Yang | Gu Gu | Daisy | Gao Gao |

2 Read and write.

1   My dad's the ___tallest___ (tall) in our family.

2   The _____ (big) animal in the world is the blue whale.

3   Lily's the _____ (good) singer in the class.

4   The dolphin is one of the _____ (smart) animals in the world.

5   My uncle Peter's the _____ (thin) grown-up in my family.

6   Daisy has the _____ (curly) hair in the class.

7   My cousin Jim thinks that Monday is the _____ (bad) day of the week.

8   My aunt's the _____ (funny) person in our family.

1 **Write the words.**

1 evom — _move_
2 pjmu — _____
3 blicm — _____
4 lafl — _____
5 iedh — _____
6 esol — _____
7 kwal — _____
8 nur — _____
9 ylf — _____

2 **Read and write a check (✓) or an ✗.**

1

✓

The lion's running.

2

☐

The panda's falling.

3

☐

The dolphin's jumping.

4

☐

The bear's climbing a tree.

5

☐

The bat's flying.

6

☐

The rabbit's hiding behind a rock.

1 Look at picture A. Read and write *yes* or *no*.

1 The bat's eating fruit below the fruit tree. ___no___

2 There's a brown bear close to a rock. _____

3 The gray bear's behind the brown bear. _____

4 The bat's across from the monkey. _____

5 The snake is in the tree. _____

6 The parrot is above the tree. _____

2 Write about the differences. Use these words.

above   across from   below   close to

1 In picture A, the monkey is above the bat, but in picture B, the monkey is below the bat.

2 _____

3 _____

4 _____

5 _____

6 _____

1 **Give the animals the correct food.**

2 **Read and match.**

1   These animals only eat plants.   a   Omnivores
2   These animals only eat meat.   b   Herbivores
3   These animals eat meat and plants.   c   Carnivores

3 **Look at the pictures. Complete the sentences.**

1 This is _a bear_ . It eats _meat and_
   plants . It is _an omnivore_ .

2 This is _____ .
   It eats _____ .
   It is _____ .

3 _____
   _____ .

4 _____
   _____ .

4 **Read and guess the animal. Draw.**

It lives in Africa.

It is a herbivore.

It eats grass and leaves.

It is big and gray.

It has four legs, big ears, and a long trunk.

It can swim, and it can run very fast.

What is it?

It is _____ .

5 **Write about your favorite wild animal. Draw.**

Name: _____   Group: _____

Color: _____   Lives: _____

Characteristics: It has _____ .

It is _____ .

It can _____ but it cannot _____ .

Food: _____

1 **Put the pictures in order. Then tell the story.**

a

b

c

d

e

f  1

2 **Choose a picture from Activity 1. Write a sentence. Read it to a friend. Can they guess which picture it is?**

It's a sunny day. A kangaroo is close to the river. She is playing with her joey.

3 **Look at the pictures. Talk about what is happening.**

1

2

3

The little boy can't swim. His dad is helping him.

Text type: An Australian dreamtime story

4 **Look at the pictures. Talk about the differences.**

In picture A, the kangaroo has a baby. In picture B, it doesn't have a baby.

5 **Ask and answer.**

Do you have a pet?

Yes, I have a cat.

1 Do you have a pet?

2 What do you do with your pet?

3 What's your favorite animal?

4 Tell me about your favorite animal.

1 Read the text and choose the best answer.

Example

Jim: Are you watching a movie, Vicky?
Vicky: (A) Yes, I am.
       B   Yes, I can.
       C   Yes, I do.

Questions

1 Jim: Is the movie about a kangaroo?
   Vicky: A   I know it is!
           B   That's right. It's great!
           C   It likes jumping!

2 Jim: Is the movie funny?
   Vicky: A   Yes, it is.
           B   Yes, it did.
           C   Yes, it can.

3 Jim: I'd like to go to the theater to see a movie.
   Vicky: A   Me, too.
           B   I liked the movie.
           C   You would go.

4 Jim: Which movie would you like to see at the theater?
   Vicky: A   You can see good movies there.
           B   I saw a good one last week.
           C   There's one about bears on this week.

5 Jim: Should we go on Saturday afternoon?
   Vicky: A   Good idea!
           B   So should I!
           C   OK, you go.

6 Jim: Why don't we ask Clare to come with us?
   Vicky: A   Let's watch this together!
           B   OK, let's do that!
           C   Why doesn't he come?

1 Play the game.

The bats are sleeping.

INSTRUCTIONS

1 Roll the die and move your marker.

2 Say what the animals are doing.

6 Our weather

My unit goals

| Practice | Say and write  new words in English | Learn to say in English |

My mission diary

	Hooray!	OK	Try again
1			
2			
3			
★			

My favorite stage: _____

Go to page 134 and add to your word stack!

I can talk about the weather.

I can use *was* and *were* to talk about the past.

I can spell clothes words.

I can listen for names, numbers, and other information.

1 **Write the words, then match.**

> clouds   rainbow   ~~raining~~   snowing   sunny   windy

1   We can't go for a walk in the country because the weather's terrible. It's <u>raining</u>.

2   It's cold and snows a lot in the mountains. It's _____ today.

3   We can fly our kites at the beach today. It's _____, and it isn't raining. Great!

4   Look, Mom, there's a _____ over the roof of that house.

5   Can we go for a swim in the lake, Dad? It's hot and _____.

6   Let's go for a long walk in the forest. It isn't hot; there are a lot of _____.

a 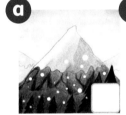 **b**  **c**  1 **d**  **e**  **f**

Sounds and spelling

How do we write that sound?

2 🎧 5.26 **Listen and point. Then listen again and say.**

3 🎧 5.27 **Listen and color the letters that make the /iː/ sound.**

> tree bee three

> windy sunny cloudy

The Friendly Farm

1 🎧 5.28 **Listen, read, and correct.**

1   Oh, my hair! It was sunny yesterday and it wasn't ~~hot~~.   cold

2   Today, I don't know, but yesterday they were in the forest. _____

3   They were on vacation in the rain. _____

4   I was with my younger cousin, and we were out in the fields. _____

5   We were in the snow, but we weren't cold. We were sad. _____

6   Look! It's cloudy, and there's a rainbow! _____

2 **Ask and answer the questions.**

1   Where were Grandma and Grandpa yesterday?

2   What was the weather like?

3   Where were Gracie and her cousin in her story?

4   What was the weather like?

5   Were they happy?

Where were Grandma and Grandpa yesterday?   In the mountains.

1 Read and circle the correct words.

1 It *wasn't* / *weren't* cloudy yesterday. It was windy.

2 Where *was* / *were* they at nine o'clock this morning?

3 I *was* / *were* in the forest with my grandparents last Sunday.

4 Where *was* / *were* she last Wednesday?

5 Why *was* / *were* your socks in the dining room?

6 You *wasn't* / *weren't* at school last Thursday.

7 He *was* / *were* in the bathroom at seven o'clock.

8 The children *wasn't* / *weren't* hot because the window *was* / *were* open.

2 Read and write the words. Answer the questions.

~~was~~   was   wasn't   were   were   weren't

Last weekend was amazing. On Saturday, I ¹ __was__ at the beach with my family. We were there all day. It was windy, but it ² _____ cold. Dad was very happy because the weather was good for flying our new kite. We were on the sand, but we ³ _____ close to the sea, and the kite was above our heads. It was very funny, because two silly birds ⁴ _____ above our heads, too. One big one ⁵ _____ below the kite, and another smaller one was above it. They ⁶ _____ happy, playing with the kite.

1 Where were they on Saturday? _____ They were at the beach. _____

2 What was the weather like? _____

3 Why was Dad very happy? _____

4 Why was it funny? _____

5 Where were the birds? _____

1 Put the words in groups.

> balcony   basement   bat   bear   ~~boots~~   cloud   coat
> floor   parrot   rabbit   rain   roof   scarf   shorts   snow
> stairs   sunny   sweater   whale   wind

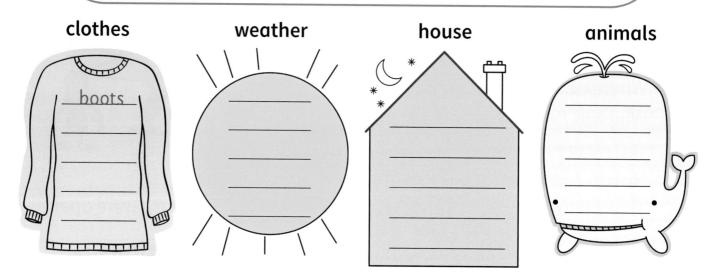

clothes

boots
_____
_____
_____
_____

weather

_____
_____
_____
_____

house

_____
_____
_____
_____
_____

animals

_____
_____
_____
_____

2 Write the words. Find the secret word.

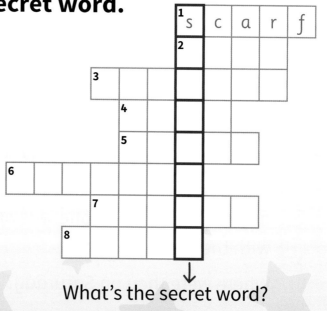

1   It's very cold today. He's wearing his long green ___scarf___.

2   Sorry, Sally. You can't _____ your pop star costume to school.

3   _____ _____ your boots in the house! They're dirty!

4   You need a hat, scarf, and _____ because it's cold outside.

5   I _____ _____ my socks before my shoes.

6   She wants to wear her pirate _____ to the party.

What's the secret word?

_____

7   When it's hot, we wear a T-shirt and _____.

8   They must put on their _____ to play in the rain.

Crossword:
1 s c a r f

1 Write the words in the correct order.

1 TV last night / a great / movie on / There was / .

   There was a great movie on TV last night.

2 any leaves / Were / on the trees / there / ?

   _____

3 a rainbow above / was / the field / There / .

   _____

4 wasn't / the farm / There / a lake opposite / .

   _____

5 at the party but / There were / only one pirate / two clowns / .

   _____

2 Read the text and choose the best answer.

1 Where were you yesterday?
   a   Yes, that's right.
   b   It was nine o'clock.
   c   I was at home.

2 What was on TV?
   a   It was windy.
   b   A movie about animals.
   c   My uncle wasn't at home.

3 Were there any bears in the movie?
   a   No, it wasn't.
   b   Yes, there was.
   c   Yes, there were.

4 What kind of bears were they?
   a   Pandas are black and white.
   b   They were big brown bears.
   c   My cousin has a teddy bear.

1 Read and match.

rain gauge

weather vane

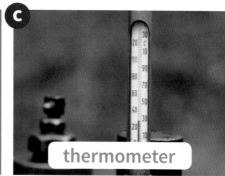
thermometer

1 This instrument measures how hot or how cold it is. ☐

2 This instrument measures how much rain falls. ☐

3 This instrument shows us the direction of the wind. ☐

2 Make a weather vane.

cardboard ☐

a straw ☐

a pin ☐

a pencil with an eraser on the end ☐

scissors ☐

colored pencils or markers ☐

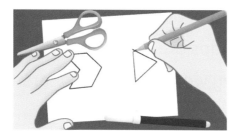

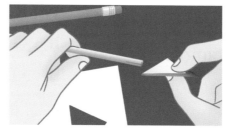

1 Draw the head and tail of the weather vane. Decorate them and cut them out.

2 Cut both ends of the straw and put the head in one end and the tail in the other.

3 Push the pin through the straw and into the eraser of the pencil.

4 Go outside and find the direction of the wind. Have fun!

3 **Draw a weather map. Then write.**

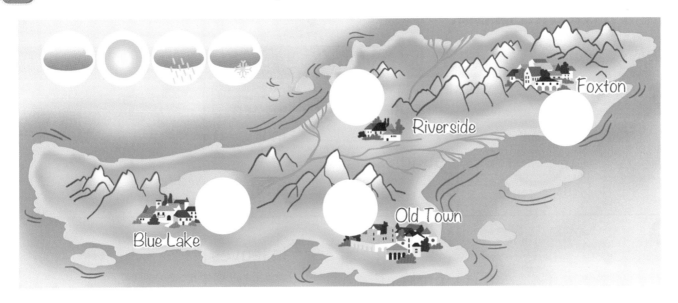

1 It is _____ in Old Town.   3 _____

2 It is _____ in Blue Lake.   4 _____

4 **Ask and answer questions about your map with a friend.**

> What's the weather like in Foxton on your island?

> It's sunny. What's the weather like in Foxton on your island?

> It's raining.

5 **Record the weather. Draw the symbols. Then talk with a friend.**

Monday	Tuesday	Wednesday	Thursday	Friday

> Was it sunny on Monday?

> Yes, it was!

1 **Complete the chart with information from the poem. Write and draw.**

Type of weather	Things to do	Type of clothes
1 rain	Imagine you are ___at sea___ _____ in the puddles. _____ a lot.	
2 _____	_____ in leaves and _____ them around.	
3 _____	_____ things in the clouds.	
4 _____	Slide on _____ . Make a _____ .	

2 **What clothes do you wear when it's warm and sunny?**

_____

3 **What can you do when it's sunny? Complete the poem.**

The sun is shining all around,

It shines on you and me.

I'm _____ .

I'm _____ , too!

I'm having fun in the sun.

How about you?

4 **Read the text. Choose the right words and write them on the lines.**

Clouds

On planet Earth, there ¹ _____are_____ lots of different kinds of clouds in the sky. Some clouds are white, fat, and fluffy. They are big, and they are high in the sky. Other kinds of clouds are gray or thin. Sometimes, they are so low we think we can touch them. ² _____ clouds contain water. The water falls as rain, but ³ _____ it is very cold, the water in the clouds freezes and falls down as ⁴ _____ .

Watching clouds is lots of fun. ⁵ _____ we can see dragons or turtles or other shapes. They also tell us what kind of weather is ⁶ _____ . For example, scientists say that green clouds mean that a tornado is coming.

1	is	are	am
2	All	Any	Every
3	what	why	when
4	snow	wind	rain
5	Never	Always	Sometimes
6	come	comes	coming

1 🎧 5.29 Listen and look. There is one example.

Go to my grandparents' house

Go at: _____12_____ o'clock

1   Road number: I- _____   4   Play with: _____

2   Video call name: Kitty _____   5   In the afternoon: Fix _____

3   In the green bag: _____

2 🎧 5.30 Listen and draw lines. There is one example.

(Ben)   (Kim)   (Ann)   (Matt)

(Julia)   (Paul)   (Hugo)

6

1 Play the game.

It was hot and sunny.

INSTRUCTIONS

1 Roll the die.
2 Move your marker.

3 Pictures: Say what you see.
4 Sentences: Read, find, and move to that space.

Review ••• Units 5–6

Name	Weather		Where		Clothes	
1 Sally	a	b	a	b	a	b
2 Jane	a	b	a	b	a	b
3 Tony	a	b	a	b	a	b
4 Fred	a	b	a	b	a	b

2 **Compare two animals. Use the words from the box.**

climb   fly   jump   run   swim   walk
smart   fast   fat   pretty   short   slow   tall   thin

Bat and panda.

A bat can fly, but a panda can't.

A panda is fatter than a bat.

3 Read and draw.

Look at my animal picture. The whale is the biggest animal. It's in the middle of the picture. There's a dolphin above the whale. It's not as big as the whale, but it's bigger than the penguin. The penguin is below the whale. The smallest animal in my picture is close to the penguin. It's a bat. There is a rabbit next to the bat.

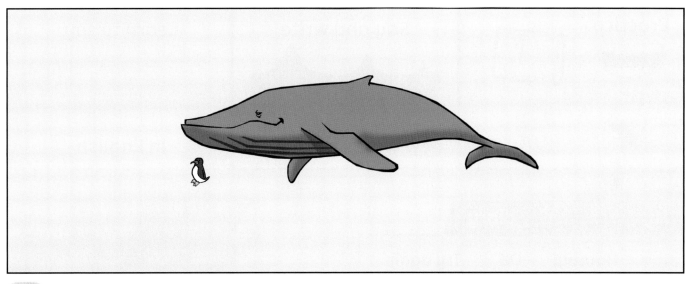

4 Write about you.

1 What's your favorite kind of weather? Why?

_____

2 What's your favorite piece of clothing? Describe it.

_____

3 What's your favorite animal?

_____

4 What does your favorite animal look like?

_____

5 What can your favorite animal do?

_____

7 Let's cook!

My unit goals

Practice

Say and write

 8 **10** **12**

new words in English

Learn to say

in English

My mission diary

	Hooray!	OK	Try again
1			
2			
3			
★			

My favorite stage: _____

Go to page 134 and add to your word stack!

☐ I can name kinds of food.

☐ I can talk and write about cooking.

☐ I can talk about things that happened in the past.

☐ I can say which picture is different and why.

7

1 Write the words.

¹ v e g e t a b l e s

Sounds and spelling

2 🎧 5.32 Listen and repeat. Match the words with the pictures.

~~armchair~~ cheese chicken chocolate

How do we say these letters?

ch

armchair

3 🎧 5.33 Listen and say the tongue twister.

Richie likes eating **ch**icken, **ch**eese, and **ch**ocolate in his arm**ch**air!

1 🎧 5.34 **Listen, read, and write.**

1

Did they bring the _food_ home?

2

They ate it all at school: soup, sandwiches, pasta, _____.

3

Yes, I saw them in the _____ yesterday, but I didn't see the food.

4

Did they go _____?

5

They got vegetables for _____.

6

What did you _____ in the soup, Gracie?

2 **Ask and answer questions. Use the words from the box.**

drink   eat   have   make

Did they eat the food at home?

No, they didn't.

1 **Write the sentences in the negative.**

1 The children had lunch in the kitchen.

The children ___didn't have___ lunch at school.

2 Fred went to the store to buy some vegetables.

Fred _____ to the store to buy a sandwich.

3 Charlie and Sally had a big, cheese sandwich at one o'clock.

Charlie and Sally _____ soup at one o'clock.

4 Jane drank orange juice with her breakfast.

Jane _____ water with her breakfast.

5 Peter made pasta for dinner.

Peter _____ pasta for lunch.

2 **Read the code and write the text.**

	A	B	C	D	E	F
1	last	her	Daisy	potatoes	she	to
2	went	carrot	stores	for	fantastic	carrots
3	was	Saturday	the	were	made	very
4	and	soup	parents	got	lunch	happy

A1 – B3 – C1 – E3 – E4 – D2 – B1 – C4. E1 – A2 – F1 – C3 – C2 – A4 – D4 – F2 –
A4 – D1. E1 – E3 – B2 – B4. B1 – C4 – D3 – F3 – F4. C3 – B4 – A3 – E2.

Last Saturday, Daisy _____

_____

_____

A cup is something you use.

1 Circle the one that doesn't belong. Say why.

1 funny	happy	cup	fantastic
2 wash	soup	pasta	salad
3 kick	drop	hit	sandwich
4 cut	sad	bad	terrible
5 cook	carry	cut	glass
6 aunt	parent	carry	son
7 bottle	drop	cup	bowl
8 cook	boil	plate	fry

2 5.35 Listen and color.

1 Write the verbs in the past.

~~boil~~ ~~bounce~~ ~~carry~~ ~~clap~~ cook copy cry drop fry hop
invite laugh like skate skip smile start stop try wash

+ed	y +ied	+d	consonant +ed
boiled	carried	bounced	clapped

2 Complete the sentences.

1 The children __washed__ their hands before dinner.

2 Last week, I _____ my friends to my birthday party.

3 Sally _____ at the camera and her dad got a good picture.

4 The movie was very funny. We all _____ a lot.

5 I helped my grandma with the groceries. I _____ the bags.

6 Peter's mom wasn't very happy because he _____ one of her favorite plates.

7 The book was very sad. I _____ at the end.

8 The rain _____ at four o'clock in the afternoon, and the children went outside to play.

1 Look and write the words.

~~flower~~   fruit   leaf   seeds

1   _flower_

2   _____

3   _____

4   _____

2 Which part of the plant do we eat?

flowers   fruit   ~~leaves~~   seeds

1   _leaves_

2   _____

3   _____

4   _____

3 Color the food from plants in green and the food from animals in red.

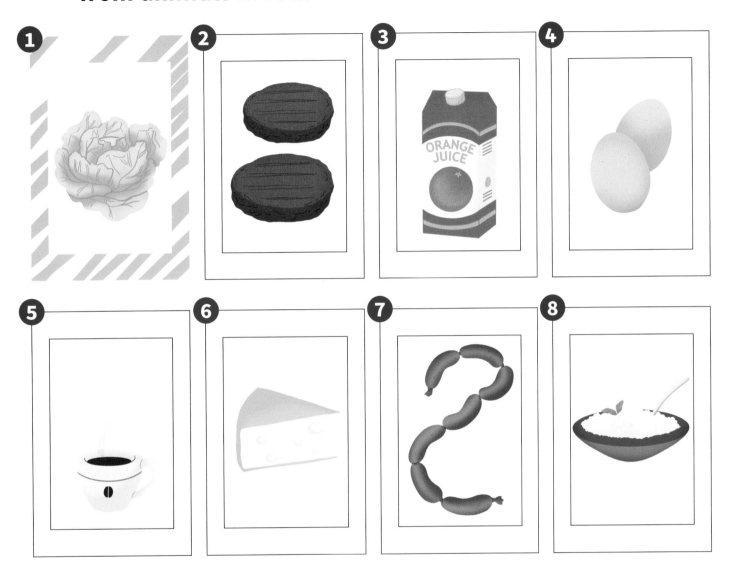

4 Read and match.

1 We use aloe vera   a   they give us oxygen.

2 We use trees   b   to make sunblock.

3 We use cotton plants   c   are medicines.

4 When plants make their food,   d   to make clothes.

5 Many plants   e   to make paper.

1 Look and read. Write *yes* or *no*. Explain your answers.

1 Sonny cooks in Uncle Raymond's café.

  <u>no</u> <u>He washes plates, bowls, cups, and glasses.</u>

2 The cooks from the café were all at home.

3 Uncle Raymond doesn't think Sonny can cook in the café.

4 Selina Redman asks Uncle Raymond to cook in her restaurant.

2 Look at the picture. What happens next? Check (✓) the best answer.

a Sonny doesn't work in Restaurant Redman. ☐

b Sonny goes to work at Restaurant Redman. Selina is very happy. ☐

c Sonny goes to work at Restaurant Redman. Selina isn't very happy. ☐

3 Ask and answer with a friend.

1 Do you like cooking?

2 What is your favorite thing to cook?

3 What is your favorite thing to eat?

Do you like cooking?   Yes, I do.

4 Read and write the words.

My name is Sonny Miller, and I am a ¹ ___chef___ . I work in Restaurant Redman every Saturday, and I love it! I make pasta, soup, and salad. I work very hard. When Selina Redman asked me to work in her restaurant, I was very ² _____ . Selina is a fantastic chef. I always go to her restaurant for my ³ _____ . She makes beautiful cakes!

I don't see Selina very often at the restaurant. She is usually in New York making her ⁴ _____ show. Do you know it? It's called *In My Kitchen*. I watch it every week! I want to have my own TV show one day.

Before I became a chef, I ⁵ _____ dishes in my Uncle Raymond's cafe. I didn't like doing that. I love ⁶ _____ , but I don't like washing dirty bowls, cups, and glasses!

sad

~~chef~~

washed

bought

birthday

happy

cooking

TV

1 🎧 5.36 **Which picture is different?**

1

2

  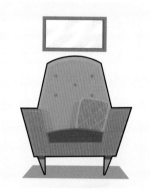 

3

4

1 Play the game.

INSTRUCTIONS

1 Roll the die and move your marker.
2 Say what the people and animals did.

What did he do?

He made a sandwich.

8 Around town

My unit goals

Practice	Say and write	Learn to say
	⭐8 ⭐10 ⭐12	
	new words in English	in English

My mission diary

	Hooray!	OK	Try again
1	🙂	😐	😕
2	🙂	😐	😕
3	🙂	😐	😕
⭐	🙂	😐	😕

My favorite stage: _____

Go to page 134 and add to your word stack!

I can write about a trip.

I can name places in a town.

I can talk about things I have to do.

I can listen and choose the correct picture.

1 Read and match.

> amusement park   ~~downtown~~   map   parking lot
> ride   road   ticket   train station

1 The part of a city where the stores are. _downtown_

2 We go there to go on fantastic rides. _____

3 We have to buy one to catch a bus or train. _____

4 You go there to catch a train. _____

5 This is a place for your car close to the stores. _____

6 We go on this at the amusement park. _____

7 Cars drive on this. It's bigger than a street. _____

8 We can use this to find places in a city. _____

Sounds and spelling

> How do we write that sound?

2 🎧 5.37 **Can you hear the /əʊ/ sound? Listen and say *yes* or *no*.**

3 🎧 5.38 **Listen and color the letters that make the /əʊ/ sound.**

snow
rainbow
grown-up

road
coat

The Friendly Farm

1  5.39 **Listen, read, write a check (✓) or an X.**

1 Grandpa Friendly bought his hat last weekend.   **X**

2 The family drove to the beach and were there for a week.

3 Henrietta and Rocky rode in Grandpa's truck. They sat next to him.

4 Grandpa Friendly brought Gracie home.

5 Grandpa Friendly gave them nice vegetables to eat.

6 Grandpa Friendly gave Harry his hat.

2 **Read and complete the story with the words from the box.**

> bought   chose   ~~found~~   gave   told   took   wore

Harry ¹ _found_ Grandpa Friendly's hat in the box. Grandpa ² _____ it last year, and he ³ _____ it on vacation at the beach. He ⁴ _____ a green one because it's his favorite color. Harry ⁵ _____ the other animals that Grandpa ⁶ _____ him the hat, but he didn't. Harry ⁷ _____ it from the yard.

1 Read and match. Color.

1 How many pictures did Jane take?

4 Which ice cream did Mary choose?

They gave me some skates.

He fed them at eight o'clock.

2 What did your grandparents give you?

5 What time did Jim feed the fish?

It slept in the yard.

She took five.

3 Where did the rabbit sleep?

6 What did Daisy's parents buy her?

She chose chocolate.

They bought her a new sweater.

2 Complete the sentences in the past.

1   Peter ___drew___ (draw) a picture for his mother.

2   Lily _____ (find) a scarf on the bus.

3   He _____ (lose) his kite in the park.

4   Fred's dad _____ (buy) five tickets.

5   Sally _____ (wear) her new yellow boots.

6   Paul's mom _____ (drive) him to school.

7   My cousin _____ (hide) behind the bookcase.

8   Charlie's friends _____ (give) him an incredible book.

9   I _____ (take) lots of pictures on vacation.

10   We _____ (go) on the biggest ride at the amusement park.

1 Write the words. Find the secret word.

| 1 | s | q | u | a | r | e |

2

3

4

5

6

7

8

9

10

11

What is the secret word? _____

2 Complete the sentences. Use the words in Activity 1.

1   Jane and her mom sat under a tree in the __square__ and fed the birds.

2   Daisy found some great adventure books in the _____.

3   Sally's uncle bought some vegetables at the _____.

4   They went to the _____ _____ and bought some new clothes.

5   Vicky's aunt had a baby boy. Vicky went to the _____ to see her new cousin.

6   Charlie and his dad went to a _____ downtown. They drank lemonade.

7   Lily and her friends went to the _____ _____ to see a movie.

8   The bus came into the _____ _____ at six o'clock.

8

1 **Read the text and complete the sentences.**

Vicky went to her grandparents' house at the beach last weekend. On Friday night, her grandfather said, "Let's go to the amusement park tomorrow. We have to get up at six o'clock, because we have to catch the number 27 bus."

"We don't have to take food because there's a café across from the amusement park," her grandmother told them.

"That's good," her grandfather said, "because I don't have to carry a big picnic basket on the rides!" Grandma and Vicky both laughed.

1 Vicky's grandfather wanted to take her to the _amusement park_ .

2 They had to _____ at six o'clock to catch the bus.

3 They didn't have to take food because there was a _____ across from the amusement park.

4 Her grandfather was happy because he didn't have to carry a picnic basket on the _____ .

2 **Write the words in the correct order.**

1 Peter has to / to school / the eight o'clock train / catch / .

Peter has to catch the eight o'clock train to school.

2 have to / seven o'clock / Mary doesn't / get up at / .

_____

3 wear a / Sally / helmet on her bike / has to / .

_____

4 My parents / do homework / have to / don't / .

_____

5 for tests / Do you / study / have to / ?

_____

1 Look and write the words.

crosswalk   road   ~~road signs~~   sidewalk
streetlight   traffic lights   trash can

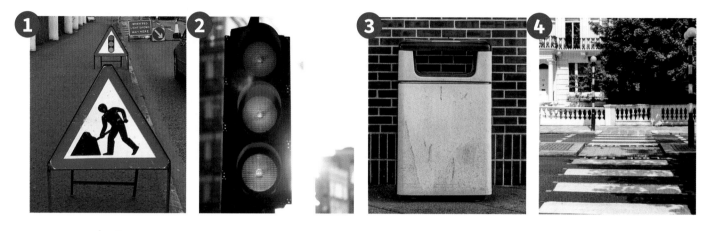

1 road signs
2 _____
3 _____
4 _____

5 _____
6 _____
7 _____

2 How can we keep safe in the city? Read and match.

1 Always walk   a   a ball close to traffic.
2 Use a crosswalk   b   the crosswalk.
3 Wait for the "WALK" sign at   c   look, listen, and think.
4 Remember to stop,   d   on the sidewalk.
5 Hold hands with a grown-up   e   to cross the road.
6 Don't play with   f   when crossing the road.

3 Read and complete. Then match.

crosswalk   look   ~~road~~   sidewalk

1   You must not play in the _____road_____ .

2   You must walk on the _____.

3   You must cross at the _____.

4   You must _____ both ways when you cross.

4 How safe are you? Circle your answers.

1	I walk on the sidewalk.	Always	Sometimes	Never
2	I use the crosswalk.	Always	Sometimes	Never
3	I run across the road.	Always	Sometimes	Never
4	I wait for the "WALK" sign before I cross the road.	Always	Sometimes	Never
5	I hold my parents' hands when we cross the road.	Always	Sometimes	Never
6	I play with a ball on the sidewalk.	Always	Sometimes	Never

1 Answer the questions.

1 Why did Tom's mom give him a little push?

Because he didn't want to

go on the bus.

2 What was the bus driver's name?

_____

_____

3 Who was Tom's bus buddy?

_____

_____

4 What could the bus do?

_____

5 What could Tom see from the bus?

_____

6 Who did Tom see at the end of the story?

_____

2 What can you learn from the story? Check (✓) the best answer.

a School buses are great. ☐

b Don't be scared to try new things. ☐

c Bus buddies are very helpful. ☐

3 **Read the text and complete the sentences.**

"Can we go to the safari park on my birthday, please?" said Tom. As they drove into the park Tom read the sign.

"Do not feed the animals."

"Why can't we feed the animals?" he asked.

"Because they are wild animals. They're not pets," his dad said.

1 Tom wanted to go to the safari park on his _birthday_ .

2 The sign said do not _____ the animals.

3 Tom's dad said it was because they were _____ animals.

The car in front stopped. The window opened, and a little girl's hand dropped a sandwich out of the window.

"Mom, look at the monkey. It wants to eat the sandwich," said Tom.

Suddenly, there were a lot of monkeys jumping on the car.

That was the day Tom learned that it is very important to read the signs.

4 He saw a little girl drop a _____ out of the window.

5 Lots of monkeys _____ on the car.

6 The little girl got into trouble because she _____ read the signs.

1 🎧 5.40 Listen and check (✓) the box. There is one example.

Where is Peter going with his mother?

a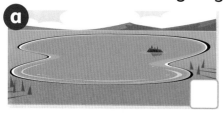

b  ✓

c

1 Which girl is Mr. Ball's granddaughter?

a

b

c

2 Which sweater does Sam want to wear to the party?

a

b

c

3 Where was Zoe on Monday?

a

b

c

4 What is Fred doing now?

a

b

c

5 Which is the new building in the city?

a

b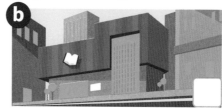

c

1 Play the game.

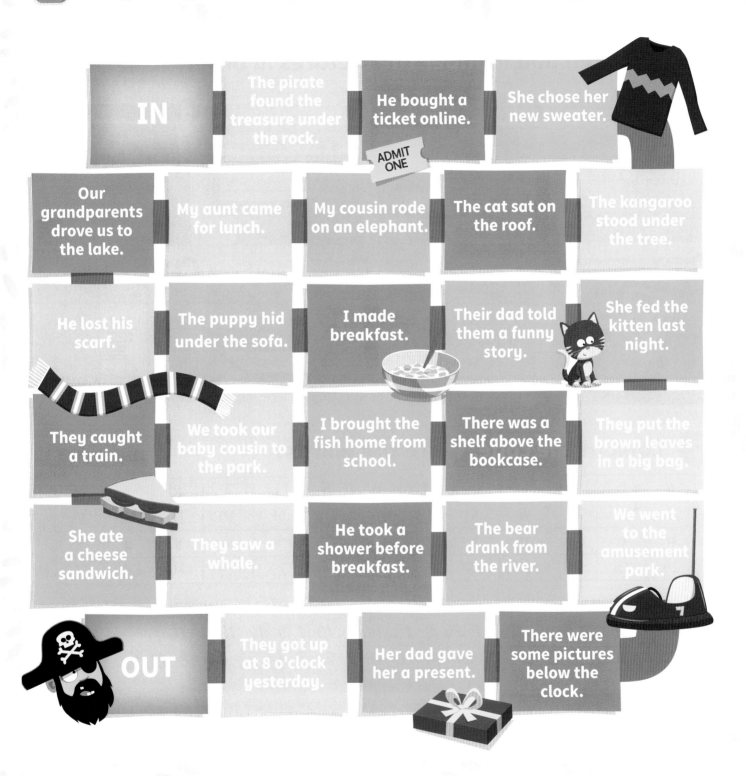

IN

The pirate found the treasure under the rock.

He bought a ticket online.

She chose her new sweater.

Our grandparents drove us to the lake.

My aunt came for lunch.

My cousin rode on an elephant.

The cat sat on the roof.

The kangaroo stood under the tree.

He lost his scarf.

The puppy hid under the sofa.

I made breakfast.

Their dad told them a funny story.

She fed the kitten last night.

They caught a train.

We took our baby cousin to the park.

I brought the fish home from school.

There was a shelf above the bookcase.

They put the brown leaves in a big bag.

She ate a cheese sandwich.

They saw a whale.

He took a shower before breakfast.

The bear drank from the river.

We went to the amusement park.

OUT

They got up at 8 o'clock yesterday.

Her dad gave her a present.

There were some pictures below the clock.

INSTRUCTIONS

1 Roll the die and move your marker.
2 Make the sentence negative.

> The pirate didn't find the treasure under the rock.

Review ••• Units 7–8

1 🎧 5.41 Listen and number the pictures in order.

2 Look at the code. Write the words.

a	b	c	d	e	f	g	h	i	j	k	l	m
1	2	3	4	5	6	7	8	9	10	11	12	13
n	o	p	q	r	s	t	u	v	w	x	y	z
14	15	16	17	18	19	20	21	22	23	24	25	26

(18 9 4 5) 19 20 1 20 9 15 14 5 13 1 9 12 13 1 16
20 18 9 16 20 5 24 20 20 18 1 22 5 12 23 15 18 12 4

1 ___ride___   2 _____   3 _____   4 _____

5 _____   6 _____   7 _____   8 _____

3 Use the code. Dictate a word to your friend.

13 1 4 5   Is it "made"?

4 **Talk about Sally and Jack. Ask and answer with a friend.**

	Make lunch?	Wash vegetables?	Fry onions?	Cook pasta?	Cut bread?	Cut cheese?
Sally	✓	✓	✓	✗	✓	✗
Jack	✓	✗	✗	✓	✓	✓

Did Sally make lunch?

Yes, she did.

5 **Complete the sentences.**

1  I went to the _____ to _____ .

2  I went to the _____ to _____ .

3  I went to the _____ to _____ .

4  I went to the _____ to _____ .

5 I went to the _____ to _____ .

9 A big change

My unit goals

Practice	Say and write	Learn to say
	 8 10 12 new words in English	in English

My mission diary

	Hooray!	OK	Try again
1			
2			
3			
⭐			

My favorite stage: _____

Go to page 134 and add to your word stack!

☐ I can understand sentences about how people are feeling.

☐ I can use *more* and *most* to compare things.

☐ I can talk about vacations and adventures.

☐ I can read a story and choose the best title.

1 Write the words.

> afraid̶ boring dangerous difficult easy exciting
> hungry scared surprised thirsty tired

1 I'm __afraid__ of the dark.

2 The test was really _____. I got everything right.

3 I love adventure movies. They're really _____.

4 It's _____ to see in the dark.

5 I'm _____ of spiders. They make me afraid.

6 The movie was so _____, I fell asleep.

7 Jim slept on the train because he was very _____.

8 Daisy had to drink a glass of water because she was very _____.

9 You have to wear a helmet because skateboarding is _____.

10 Jane didn't tell her mother about the party. She was very _____.

11 Mary ate three bananas because she was very _____.

Sounds and spelling

 2 **Listen and point to the letters.**
5.42

ing | in

ing or *in?*

ing in

 3 **Listen again and complete the words.**
5.42

1 excit_ing_____   4 pengu_____

2 w_____d   5 dolph_____

3 bor_____   6 swimm_____

The Friendly Farm

1 🎧 5.43 **Listen and ⊂circle⊃ the correct words.**

1 I think your mother's more *tired* / ⊂*surprised*⊃ than me.

2 The circus is more *boring* / *exciting* than the farm!

3 Jumping and catching are *dangerous* / *easy*.

4 Circus clothes are more *difficult* / *beautiful* than these.

5 He isn't *afraid* / *hungry*.

6 We're in the Friendly Circus. I'm riding Harry. I'm not *scared* / *surprised*.

2 **Read and write the words.**

> circus   dangerous   exciting   ~~grandparents~~   rode   surprised

1 Jim and Jenny's parents told the _grandparents_ that they wanted to work for Diversicus.

2 Grandma was more _____ than Grandpa.

3 Rocky said that a circus was more _____ than a farm and he thought it was a great idea.

4 Gracie was afraid because she thought jumping and catching were more _____ than playing music.

5 The animals wanted to have a _____ in the barn.

6 Shelly sang, Cameron jumped, and Rocky _____ on Harry.

1 Write the words in the correct order.

1 skateboarding's / than roller-skating / Mary thinks / more exciting / .

   Mary thinks skateboarding's more exciting than roller-skating.

2 more dangerous / rabbits / are / than / Bears / .

   _____

3 beautiful / more / than bats / Daisy / lions / thinks that / are / .

   _____

4 Jim was / At the amusement park, / than Jenny / more scared / .

   _____

5 than riding / Jack thinks / a bike / climbing's / more difficult / .

   _____

2 Circle the word that is true for you. Tell your friend.

What do you think?

1	Horseback riding's more dangerous than climbing.	yes	no
2	Swimming's more difficult than riding a bike.	yes	no
3	Watching TV's more boring than playing outside.	yes	no
4	Parrots are more beautiful than lions.	yes	no
5	Amusement parks are more exciting than skateboarding.	yes	no

I think horseback riding is less dangerous than climbing.

1 **Find three words in a line from the same group.**

1

map	hungry	exciting
sweater	scared	world tour
dangerous	fall	adventure

2

busy	movie theater	email
drive	hospital	market
travel	library	café

3

letter	text	email
costume	cage	world tour
fry	fall	café

4

journey	map	phone
family	travel	circus
exciting	ride	trip

2 **Read the text. Choose the right words and write them on the lines.**

People enjoy ¹ _traveling_____ . They like to fly or drive around the world. Some people look ² _____ hot weather, sand, and beaches; others want to play sports. People use ³ _____ , phones, or computers to find places to go to and new things to do. They like telling ⁴ _____ friends and families about their trips. The ⁵ _____ way to do this is by text or email with their cell phones or tablets. Letters are very slow. In many towns, there are internet cafés where people can write and send ⁶ _____ to their friends in other places or countries.

1	traveled	traveling	travel
2	for	at	on
3	trips	maps	stairs
4	his	hers	their
5	easiest	easy	easier
6	falls	emails	boils

9

1 Look and read. Write *yes* or *no*.

Jim loves mountain climbing. He thinks it's the most exciting sport. Jim always climbs with his mom. His dad doesn't climb with them because he thinks it is one of the most dangerous sports.

Last year, Jim wanted to climb one of the most difficult mountains close to their town, but his mom didn't think it was the best idea. Jim fell and was very scared, but his mom helped him climb back down to the ground. His dad drove them home. They were tired, cold, and hungry. Jim learned a lot that day, and now, he chooses easier mountains to climb.

1   Jim loves mountain climbing. _____yes_____

2   He thinks it's the most boring sport. _____

3   Jim's dad thinks it's one of the most dangerous sports. _____

4   Last year, Jim wanted to climb one of the easiest mountains. _____

5   His mom thought it was the best idea. _____

6   Jim dropped his bottle of water and was very thirsty. _____

7   His father drove them home. _____

8   Now, Jim chooses easier mountains to climb. _____

2 🎧 5.44 Listen and write.

Field trip

1   Went to mountains by: _train_____

2   Name of mountains: _____ Mountains

3   Number of children: _____

4   Which animal: _____

5   What food: chicken _____

6   What drink: _____ juice

1 Color the continents.

Africa – green
Europe – yellow
Asia – orange
North America – blue
South America – red
Australia – purple
Antarctica – pink

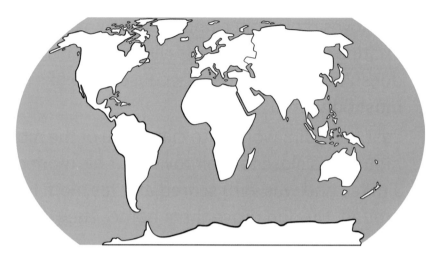

2 Look and match. Write the continent.

Great Barrier Reef   Machu Picchu   Stonehenge   Taj Mahal   ~~Victoria Falls~~

Victoria Falls Africa   _____   _____

_____   _____

3 Are these beautiful places natural or man-made?

River Amazon

_____natural_____

Stonehenge

_____

The Acropolis

_____

Mount Everest

_____

Niagara Falls

_____

The Great Wall of China

_____

4 Write sentences.

The Grand Canyon

This is _____ .

It is in _____ .

The Great Pyramid

This is _____ .

It is in _____ .

1 Read and correct.

1 The picnic was at Richard's house.

  The picnic was in the woods.

2 Richard's mother hid the clues.

  _____

3 All of the clues were in the trees.

  _____

4 There was a tree like a tiger in the woods.

  _____

5 The last clue was 90 steps from the picnic.

  _____

2 Find words that rhyme.

> around   behind   Ben   ~~do~~   eat   everyone
> giraffe   good   know   news   shiver   tree

1 two   do   7 laugh   _____
2 wood   _____ 8 see   _____
3 fun   _____ 9 clues   _____
4 ground   _____ 10 go   _____
5 find   _____ 11 river _____
6 ten   _____ 12 treat _____

3 Work in small groups. Have a treasure hunt in your classroom. Write five clues about where the secret treasure is. Follow another group's clues.

4 🎧 5.45 **Listen and check (✓) the box.**

1 What is the book about?

2 Whose party is it?

3 Where's the picnic?

4 Which competition is Ana in?

1 Read the story. Choose the correct words and write them next to numbers 1–5. There is one example.

Last week Lily and her mom went to see Lily's Uncle Pat. He lives on an
__island__ . On Saturday morning, Pat took Mom and Lily to see all the
animals, fruit, and (1) _____ in that place. Lily took lots of pictures.
"Everything is very different here," said Lily. "I want to tell Dad about this
place." "Why don't you send him an email, with some (2) _____, too?"
said Mom. In the evening, Lily wrote to her dad, but she couldn't put the
pictures from her camera into the computer. "Why don't you look for some
on the Internet?" said Mom. Lily looked at lots of different animals. "Is this a
picture of the (3) _____ we saw?" she asked. "I think it was bigger than
that, and it had a longer (4) _____," said Mom. "But ask Pat – he can
help you." "Good idea," said Lily, and she went (5) _____ to her uncle.

| lizard | pictures | tail | island | downstairs |

| vegetables | hungry | computer | pirate |

2 Now choose the best name for the story. Check (✓) one box.

Lily's Uncle Pat ☐   Lily's drawings ☐   Lily's beach ☐

1 Play the game.

Where did you go?

I went to the market.

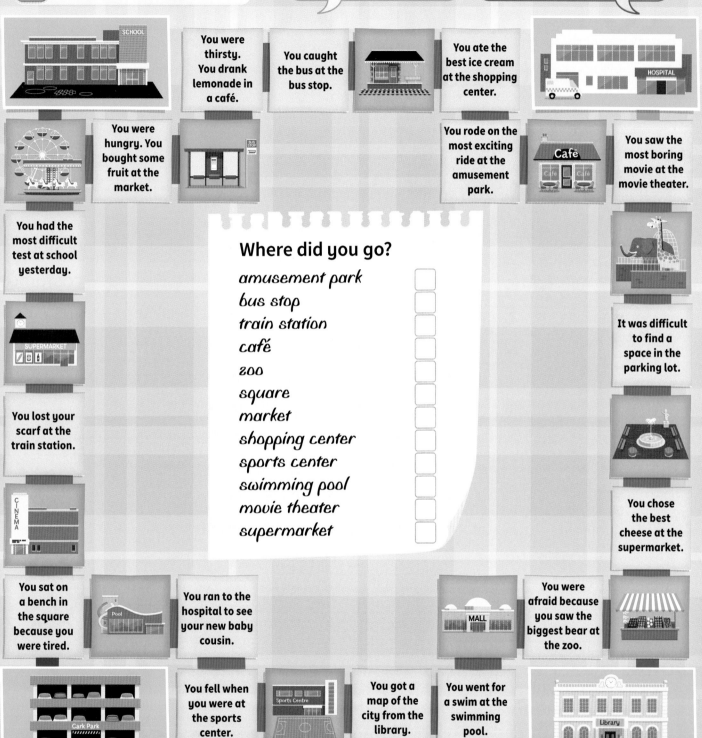

SCHOOL

You were thirsty. You drank lemonade in a café.

You caught the bus at the bus stop.

You ate the best ice cream at the shopping center.

HOSPITAL

You were hungry. You bought some fruit at the market.

BUS STOP

You rode on the most exciting ride at the amusement park.

Café

You saw the most boring movie at the movie theater.

You had the most difficult test at school yesterday.

SUPERMARKET

It was difficult to find a space in the parking lot.

You lost your scarf at the train station.

CINEMA

Where did you go?

amusement park ☐
bus stop ☐
train station ☐
café ☐
zoo ☐
square ☐
market ☐
shopping center ☐
sports center ☐
swimming pool ☐
movie theater ☐
supermarket ☐

You chose the best cheese at the supermarket.

You sat on a bench in the square because you were tired.

Pool

You ran to the hospital to see your new baby cousin.

MALL

You were afraid because you saw the biggest bear at the zoo.

Cark Park

You fell when you were at the sports center.

Sports Centre

You got a map of the city from the library.

You went for a swim at the swimming pool.

Library

INSTRUCTIONS

1 Choose a place to start.

2 Check four places on your list.

3 Roll the die and move your marker.

4 Visit the places on your list.

10 Review Unit

Units 1–3

1 Write the words.

ACROSS:

2   I take a _____ every morning.

4   She's wearing a _____ costume.

5   The _____ is tall and thin.

7   He has a mustache and a _____.

8   Do you like to read _____ books?

DOWN:

1   A ___*nurse*___ takes care of sick people.

3   You should _____ your hands before you eat.

6   I wake up at _____ o'clock.

7   _____ your teeth before you go to bed.

8   They have brown, _____ hair.

2 🎧 5.46 Listen, look, and write the day.

Sunday   Monday   Tuesday   Wednesday
Thursday   Friday   Saturday

1 _____

2 _____

3 _____

4 __Monday__

5 _____

6 _____

7 _____

3 Complete the sentences with *always*, *often*, *sometimes*, or *never*. Then ask and answer with a friend.

1 I _____ go for a swim.

2 I _____ go for a walk in the forest.

3 I _____ go shopping.

4 I _____ read books.

5 I _____ watch DVDs.

6 I _____ play soccer.

7 I _____ go roller-skating.

> How often do you go for a swim?

> I often go for a swim on Saturday.

4 Look at the pictures. Complete the sentences.

> big   black   curly   fat   long (x2)
> short (x2)   small   straight   ~~tall~~   thin

1  **2**  **3**  **4**

1   It is <u>tall</u> and _____. It has a _____ mustache.

2   It is _____ and fat. It has a _____ mustache and a _____ beard.

3   It is tall and _____. It has short, _____, blond hair and a _____ beard.

4   It is short and thin. It has _____, _____, _____ hair.

5 Read and circle *True* or *False*.

Mrs. Friendly has curly, blond hair   True   (False)

Mr. Friendly has short, black hair.   True   False

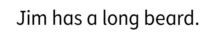
Jim has a long beard.   True   False

Jenny has straight, brown hair.   True   False

6 Match the questions with the answers.

1 Why are you a clown?

2 Why is he a dentist?

3 Why is she a doctor?

4 Why are you a farmer?

5 Why are they nurses?

a Because I like growing vegetables.

b Because they like taking care of people.

c Because she likes helping sick people.

d Because I like making people laugh.

e Because he likes fixing people's teeth.

7 Write about you. Then ask and answer with a friend.

1   What do you like to do?

I like to _____, _____, and _____.

2   What do you want to be? Why?

I want to be a/an _____ because I like _____.

What do you want to be?

I want to be a clown because I like to make people laugh.

1 🎧 5.47 **Listen and number.**

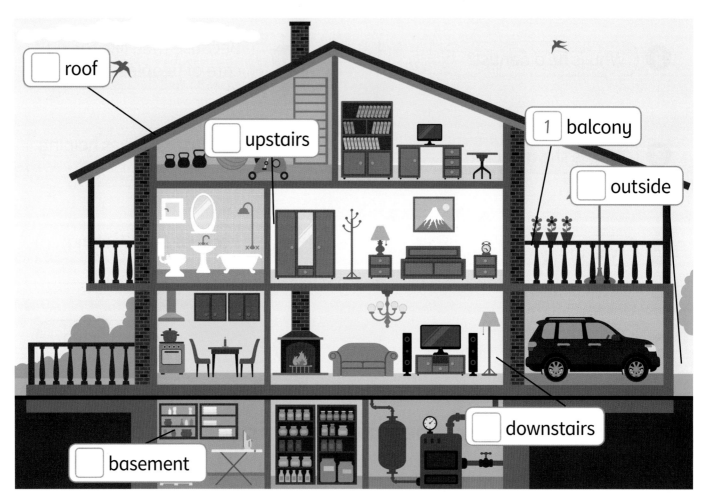

roof

upstairs

1 balcony

outside

downstairs

basement

2 **Where were they? Read and circle *was* or *were*.**

1   The cousins *was* / *were* playing outside.

2   The daughter *was* / *were* upstairs in her bedroom.

3   The grandparents *was* / *were* reading on the balcony.

4   The parents *was* / *were* cleaning the basement.

5   The son *was* / *were* downstairs in the living room.

6   The uncle *was* / *were* fixing the roof.

3 Complete the dialogue.

~~clouds~~   cold   raining   sunny   windy

Look at those gray clouds.
It's _____ and _____.
We can't go outside today.

Oh, my hair! It was _____ yesterday, and it wasn't _____.

4 Look at Activity 3. Read and circle *True* or *False*.

1	There are gray clouds above the barn.	(True)	False
2	The animals are close to the barn door.	True	False
3	Henrietta is sitting below the other animals.	True	False
4	It is raining and cold.	True	False
5	The weather was snowy yesterday.	True	False

5 Complete the chart.

Adjective	Comparative (-er / -ier)	Superlative (-est)
big	*bigger*	biggest
	faster	fastest
fat	fatter	
long		
	louder	
		oldest
quiet		
	shorter	
		slowest
small		
	thinner	
		youngest

6 Complete the sentences.

1 A dog is _____older_____ (old) than a puppy.

2 A giraffe is _____ (tall) than a horse.

3 A kitten is _____ (young) than cat.

4 A lion is _____ (big) than a mouse.

5 A parrot is _____ (small) than a penguin.

6 A sheep is _____ (fat) than a goat.

7 What animals were at the zoo? Complete the sentences.

bear   dolphin   ~~lion~~   pandas   parrots   penguins

1

There <u>was a lion</u>.

2

There _____.

3

There _____.

4

There _____.

5

There _____.

6

There _____.

8 Look at Activity 7. Answer the questions.

1 Which animal is the biggest?   The _____lion_____ is the biggest.

2 Which animal is the cutest?   _____.

3 Which animal is the loudest?   _____.

4 Which animal is the fastest?   _____.

5 Which animal is the slowest?   _____.

6 Which animal is the strongest?   _____.

Units 7–9

1 **Write the words.**

ACROSS:

1 I bought a <u>ticket</u> for the amusement park.

3 She was _____ by the party.

5 Jim _____ the cake mix.

6 He had an _____.

DOWN:

2 The woman

_____

when she cut the onions.

3 He dropped his _____ on the table.

4 The old lion was _____.

7 I poured some orange juice in a _____.

8 She _____ her ice cream.

9 The _____ bear ate a mango.

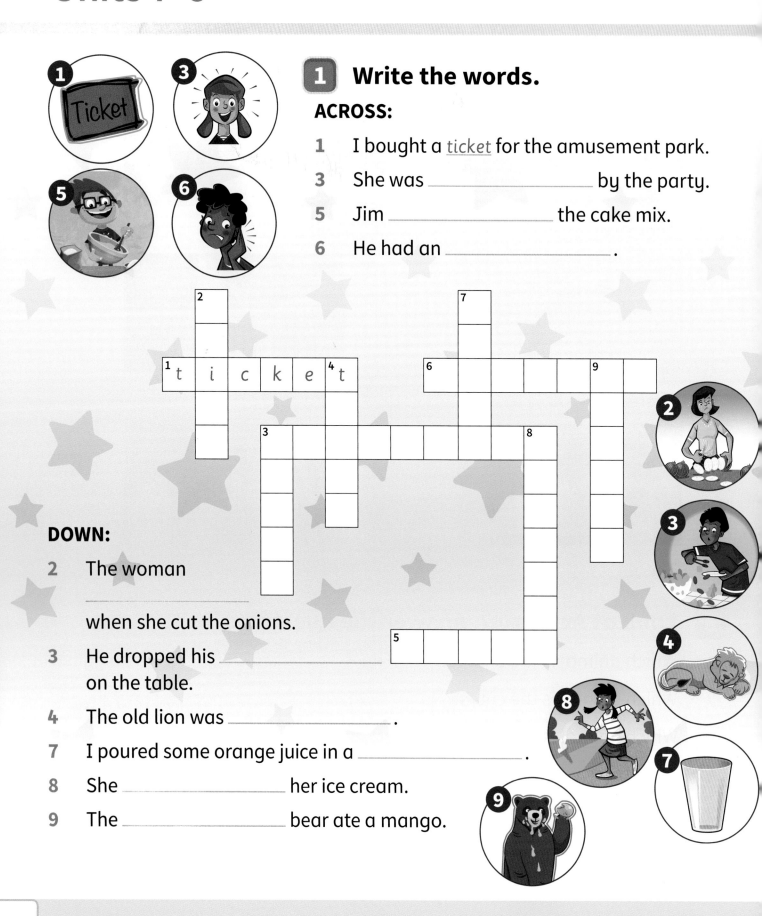

2 🎧 5.48 Listen to the story. Then number the sentences in order.

☐ Sometimes his family comes by to say "Hi" and to have some soup!

☐ He cooks soup every weekend in the town square.

☐ People take the train and ride the bus into town to have his soup.

☐ "Soup Man" makes soup to help feed hungry people.

☐ His soup is better than the soup at a café or a supermarket.

1 There is a wonderful man called the "Soup Man."

3 Write the sentences.

1 Youhavetodrivetogettothecity.   You have to drive to get to the city.

2 Wedon'thavetogetbooksatthelibrary. _____

3 Youdon'thavetouseamaptogettothecountry. _____

4 Ihavetowashthefoodandthenfryit. _____

4 **Where did they go? Follow the maze. Write and match.**

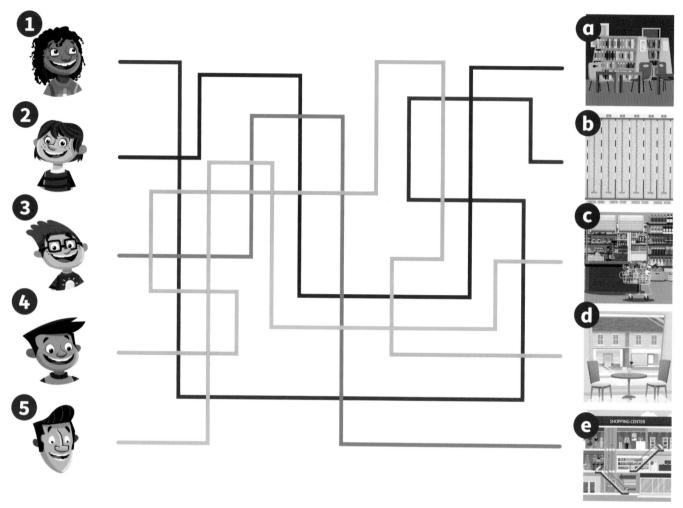

1 Eva went to the <u>swimming pool</u>   a to buy food.

2 Jenny went to the _____   b to eat lunch.

3 Jim went to the _____   c to go for a swim.

4 Tom went to a _____   d to return a book.

5 Mr. Friendly went to the _____   e to buy a new T-shirt.

5 **Ask and answer with a friend.**

Where did Eva go?

She went to the pool to go for a swim.

6 Read and correct.

1 I went to the movie theater ~~to buy food for dinner~~.   *to see a movie*

2 She went to the station <u>to see an exciting movie</u>.   _____

3 He went to the sports center <u>to make a salad</u>.   _____

4 We went to the restaurant <u>to read books</u>.   _____

7 What do you like to do in the city? Ask and answer with a friend.

What do you like to do?

I like to go and see an exciting movie.
What do you like to do?

8 Think about what you learned in Units 1–9 and answer the questions.

1 What was the most difficult thing you learned?

_____

2 What was the easiest thing you learned?

_____

3 What was the most exciting thing you learned?

_____

4 What was the most boring thing you learned?

_____

5 What was the most surprising thing you learned?

_____

1 **Write your favorite new words.**

Home Booklet

Kathryn Escribano

with Caroline Nixon and Michael Tomlinson

CAMBRIDGE
University Press

1 A day on the farm

Where's Jack swimming?

(Circle) five more words →↓. Which word completes the sentence?

m	o	u	n	t	a	i	n
t	o	r	t	r	o	c	k
o	l	l	e	a	v	e	s
c	l	a	n	c	e	a	a
p	x	k	o	t	o	n	m
a	d	e	s	o	r	t	e
n	f	t	g	r	a	s	s

Jack's swimming in the _____ .

Window to the World

The Amazon water lily is from the Amazon River in South America. Its leaves are very big. They're two meters wide!

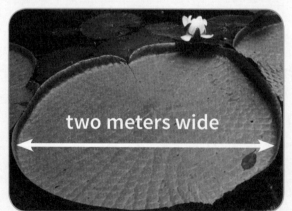

two meters wide

What's two meters wide at home? Write.

At home, the _____ is two meters wide.

Answer Jack

 What's Daisy doing?

1

She's having breakfast.

2

_____
_____

3

_____
_____

4

_____
_____

Home mission

Make a book with seven pages. Ask someone at home to help.
On the cover of your book, write "Me and my home."
Keep your book.

1
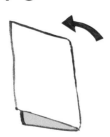

2

3

Me and
my home

Days of the week puzzle

Write the missing days!

```
            W
            E
  ¹M O N  D  A  Y
      2     N
      3     E
           ⁴S
     5      D
      6     A
            Y
```

1 ___Monday___ , _____ , and _____ have six letters.

2 _____ and _____ start with the letter "S."

3 _____ , _____ , and _____ have
the letter "t" in them.

4 _____ is my favorite day.

Window to the World

"Sunday" comes from the word "sun." and "Monday" comes from
the word "moon."

In your language, which words do "Monday" and "Tuesday" come from?

the sun   the moon

Home rules

Write Daisy's home rules. Then, write your home rules in your notebook.

> get dressed for school ~~get up early for school~~
> go to bed late   have candy for breakfast

I should ...

- brush my teeth after breakfast, lunch, and dinner.
- get up early for school .
- _____ .

I should not ...

- watch a movie before I do my homework.
- _____ .
- _____ .

Home mission

On the cover of your book, draw yourself with someone you live with, or stick a picture.
What do you do together? Write.

This is me and my sister Ana.
We listen to music on weekends.

Tongue twister

Can you say this ten times?

She goes shopping and skating on Sundays.

5

3 Party time!

Guess who

- The pop star's singing.
- The cook's making a cake.
- The farmer's riding a horse.
- The clown's taking pictures.

| clown | ~~cook~~ | farmer | pop star |

1

cook

2

_____

3

_____

4

_____

Lost objects

Read and match.

The comic book is for the tall man with short, straight, black hair. The towel is for the tall woman with short, curly, blond hair. The CD is for the tall woman with long, curly, blond hair. The present is for the short man with a beard and a mustache.

Tongue twister

Can you say this ten times?

Peter Pirate's puppy's playing.

Why are you buying that?

Write Daisy's and Jack's answers.

1
Because I want to be a pirate.

2

3

4

Window to the World

In the world, the most common hair color is black, then brown, and then blond.

What color is your hair? Is it straight or curly? Draw, color, and write.

My hair is _____ and _____ .

Home mission

Ask two people at home, "What's your favorite costume?" and write their answers. On page 1 of your book, draw a crazy costume using the answers. Write about the costume.

My dad's favorite costume is a pirate, and my brother's favorite costume is a farmer. This is a pirate-farmer costume!

4 The family at home

Jack's family pictures

Read, look, and write the numbers. They should add up to 17!

1 aunts
2
3
4
sons
5 uncle's snakes
6
7
8
cousins

1 Which aunt is shorter? _____2_____

2 Which son is taller? _____

3 Which snake is longer? _____

4 Which cousin has curlier hair? _____

_____2_____ + _____ + _____ + _____ = 17

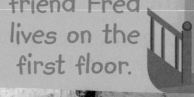

Tongue twister

Can you say this ten times?

Frank's friend Fred lives on the first floor.

What's he saying?

hers	his	~~mine~~	theirs

1. It's _mine_ .

2. It's _____ .

They're _____ .

3.

4. It's _____ .

Window to the World

The Empire State Building in New York City has 102 floors, and there are more than 1,500 steps on the stairs!

Count the steps on the stairs at home. How many are there?

The Empire State Building

Home mission

Draw someone from your family on page 2 of your book: an aunt, a cousin … Show your picture to the people you live with. Can they guess who it is?
Write about the person in the picture.

This is my aunt, Laura. She has curly … She lives in …

Animal movements!

Write the animals' names in the circles!

| ~~atbs~~ bbarits roongkaas lehwas rrtoaps philodsn |

They fly.

_____ bats _____

_____

They jump.

_____

_____

They swim.

_____

_____

Window to the World

Animals can be diurnal or nocturnal. Diurnal animals are awake in the daytime, and they sleep at night. Nocturnal animals sleep in the daytime, and they're awake at night. Penguins are diurnal, and bats are nocturnal.

Which other animals are nocturnal? Find two.

bats sleeping in the daytime

Wildlife park

Help Jack find the animals. Write.

pandas   bears   ?
?   ?   ~~lions~~
?   kangaroos   ?

Animal Kingdom Wildlife Park

1   The ___lions___ are across from the bears.
2   The lions are above the _____.
3   The kangaroos are below the _____.
4   The bears are close to the _____.

Tongue twister

Can you say this ten times?

Can kangaroos climb?

Home mission

Ask someone at home, "What's your favorite animal?" Draw the animal on page 3 of your book, or stick a picture. Write about the animal.

My mom loves pandas. They live in the mountains in China ...

Weather trail

Help Daisy get to the rainbow. Make a trail with seven more weather words.

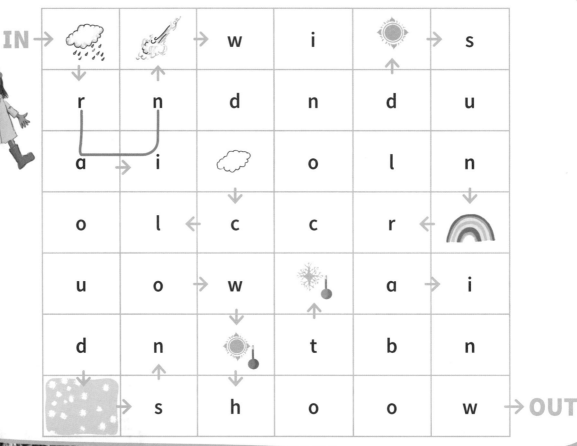

Window to the World

A rainbow happens when it's rainy in one part of the sky and sunny in another.

Learn the colors of the rainbow. Practice this sentence:

Ride on your green bike in Venice.

Match the colored letters in the sentence to the names of the colors.

[r] red [ ] green [ ] violet [ ] indigo [ ] orange [ ] blue [ ] yellow

Crazy clothes!

Look at the pictures of Daisy's bedroom. Can you complete Jack's notes?

> boots   coat   scarf   shorts   sweater   ~~T-shirt~~

Monday

Tuesday

Wednesday

Monday
It was cold, but there was a _____T-shirt_____ and _____ on the bed!

Tuesday
It was hot, but there was a _____ and a _____ on the chair!

Wednesday
There was snow, but the _____ and the _____ were behind the door!

Tongue twister

Can you say this ten times?

Walter wants windy weather.

Home mission

Describe the weather today on page 4 of your book. Then ask someone at home, "What are you wearing?" Draw the person and write.

Today, it's cold and sunny.
My dad's wearing a green sweater ...

7 Let's cook!

The best menu

Look at the menus and the food Jack and Daisy like and don't like.
Choose the best menu for them.

Menu 1	Menu 2	Menu 3	Menu 4
vegetable soup meatballs	salad hamburger	vegetable soup pasta	salad cheese sandwich

(Jack)	✗	✓	✓	✓	✓	✗
(Daisy)	✓	✓	✗	✗	✓	✓

- The best menu for Jack is number _____.
- The best menu for Daisy is number _____.

Tongue twister

Can you say this ten times?

Paula's putting the pasta on the plate.

14

Daisy or Jack?

What did Daisy and Jack do yesterday? Look, read, and write *Daisy* or *Jack*.

1

I carried the plates.

Jack

2

I washed the cups.

3

I cut the onion with my dad.

4

I dropped a glass!

Window to the World

Remember that to keep healthy, it's good to eat five portions of fruits and vegetables every day.

Which fruits and vegetables did you eat yesterday?

Look at the picture. Make your number 5 with fruits and vegetables!

Home mission

Ask three people at home, "What does your favorite sandwich have in it?" and write their answers. On page 5 of your book, draw a "super sandwich" with all the ingredients.
Write about it!

This is our super sandwich. It has cheese, chicken ...

Words for a day trip

Write the missing letters. Make a new word with those letters. What is it?

1
s _t_ ation

2
ra __ nbow

3
__ a __ e

4
mark __ __

The new word is _t_____ .

What did Jack do?

Look and answer.

1

2

3

1 Did Jack get a DVD from the library?
   No, he got a book.

2 Did Jack give Daisy a hat?
   _____

3 Did Jack buy some cake in the café?
   _____

Tongue twister

Can you say this ten times?

Ten tickets to town, please.

TICKETS

Daisy's list

Look at Daisy's list. Where does she have to go? Tell her.

bus station ~~bus station~~ library
sports center   supermarket

Monday	buy the bus tickets for school with Mom
Tuesday	buy some food for the party with Dad
Wednesday	go to my swimming class
Thursday	get some books for the weekend

On Monday, <u>you have to go to the bus station</u> .

On Tuesday, _____
_____ .

On Wednesday, _____
_____ .

On Thursday, _____
_____ .

The British Library is one of the largest libraries in the world. It has about 25 million books!

Which is the largest library in the world? Find out!

Do you sometimes go to a library? What's its name?

The British Library

Home mission

Ask three people at home, "What's your favorite place in town?" and write their answers. Choose one of the places for page 6 of your book. Draw the place or stick a picture.
Write about the place.

My grandma's favorite place in town is the sports center. She goes …

Look and write the words!

a	b	c	d	e	f	g	h	i	j	k	l	m

n	o	p	q	r	s	t	u	v	w	x	y	z

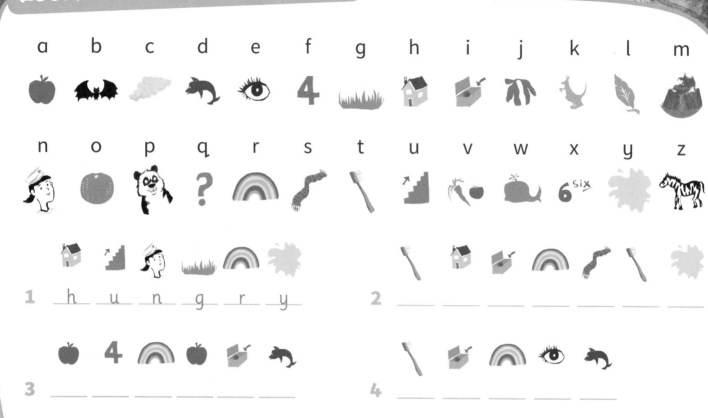

1 h u n g r y

2 _____

3 _____

4 _____

Use the code to write more words. Show them to people at home.
Can they guess the words?

Window to the World

Wiley Post was an American aviator. He went around the world in a plane in 1933 – that's more than 80 years ago! He did this in seven days, 18 hours, and 49 minutes. Now, you can fly around the world in 51 hours!

How many days are there in 51 hours? Find out!

A, B, or C?

What do you think? Look and write *A*, *B*, or *C*.

  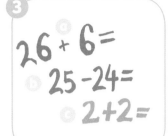 

1 ____ is more beautiful than ____ . ____ is the most beautiful.

2 ____ is more exciting than ____ . ____ is the most exciting.

3 ____ is more difficult than ____ . ____ is the most difficult.

4 ____ is more dangerous than ____ . ____ is the most dangerous.

Tongue twister

Can you say this ten times?

Here's Henry,
the hungry horse!

Home mission

Ask three people at home, "What's the most exciting place to visit?" and write their answers. Choose one of the places for page 7 of your book. Draw the place or stick a picture. Write about the place. This is the last page of your book. Congratulations!

These are the Victoria Falls in Africa. It's my dad's most exciting place to visit.

19

Country

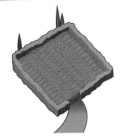
field

forest

grass

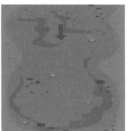
ground

lake

leaf / leaves

mountain

river

rock

tractor

 Say the name of a forest, a mountain, and a river in your country.

Daily routines

get dressed

get up

have breakfast

take a shower

toothbrush

toothpaste

towel

wake up

 What time do you … ? Choose three activities.

Days of the week

Monday

Tuesday

Wednesday

Thursday

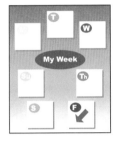
Friday

Saturday

Sunday

 Which day comes after Tuesday and before Thursday?

Free-time activities

go shopping

go skating

listen to a CD

listen to music

read a comic book

watch a DVD

watch a movie

write an email

 What do you like doing? Say three things.

Jobs and parties

clown

cook

dentist

doctor

farmer

movie star

nurse

pirate

pop star

present

treasure

  Which is your favorite costume?

Physical descriptions

beard

blond

curly

fat

light

mustache

short

straight

tall

thin

 Describe a person from your favorite TV show.

Extended family

aunt

cousin

daughter

granddaughter

grandparents

grandson

parents

son

uncle

Can you think of five more family words?

In and around the home

balcony

basement

downstairs

elevator

first floor

second floor

third floor

inside

outside

roof

stairs

upstairs

In school, which floor is your classroom on?

5

bat	bear	cage	dolphin	kangaroo	lion

panda	parrot	penguin	rabbit	whale

Can you think of five more animals?

Action verbs

climb	fall	fly	hide	jump

lose	move	run	walk

Choose five actions. Act them out!

The weather

cloud

cold

hot

rain

rainbow

snow

sunny

wind

 What's the weather like today?

Clothes

boots

coat

put on

scarf

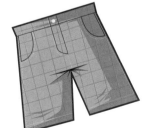
shorts

sweater

T-shirt

take off

 What are you wearing today?

25

Food

bottle bowl cheese cup glass pasta

plate salad sandwich soup vegetables

What can you drink in a glass? What can you eat in a bowl?

Actions in the kitchen

boil carry cook cry

cut drop fry wash

Do you help in the kitchen? What do you do?

A day trip

amusement park

downtown

map

parking lot

ride

road

station

ticket

trip

What's the name of an amusement park where you live?
What's your favorite ride?

Places in town

bus station

café

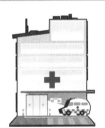
hospital

library

market

movie theater

shopping center

sports center

supermarket

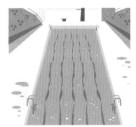
swimming pool

Choose three places. How often do you go to them?

Adjectives for opinions and feelings

afraid   boring   dangerous   difficult   easy   exciting

hungry   scared   surprised   thirsty   tired

 Choose five adjectives. Act them out!

A new adventure

adventure   busy   email   around

text / send a text   travel   world

Close your eyes. How many adventure words can you remember?

My picture dictionary

Draw and write words you know in English.

My picture dictionary

Draw and write words you know in English.

  My picture dictionary

Draw and write words you know in English.